Life And Adventures of Chickasaw, the Scout

L. H. NARON OR CHICKASAW, THE SCOUT.

Life And Adventures of Chickasaw, the Scout

The Personal Account of a Union Army Scout During the American Civil War

R. W. Surby

and

L. H. Naron

LEONAUR

Life And Adventures of Chickasaw, the Scout
The Personal Account of a Union Army Scout During the American Civil War
by R. W. Surby and L. H. Naron

First published under the title
Life And Adventures of Chickasaw, the Scout, While Serving Under the Command of
Genls. Sherman, Pope, Rosecrans, Dodge and Grierson, During the years 1861, 1862,
1863, 1864.

Leonaur is an imprint
of Oakpast Ltd

ISBN: 978-1-78282-034-5 (hardcover)
ISBN: 978-1-78282-035-2 (softcover)

http://www.leonaur.com

Publisher's Notes

Contents

Chickasaw, the Scout

The following narrative was furnished the writer by the hero of the story. He is better known in the Union army by the name of Chickasaw, and thousands can testify to his deeds while serving in the capacity of scout:

In the spring of 1861 I secretly organized three hundred Union men in Mississippi, with the promise of nine hundred more, making a full regiment. It was my intention, at this time, to place the regiment at the service of Governor Pettis, of Mississippi, for the purpose of enforcing the State of South Carolina to adhere to the Union. Some six weeks afterward an answer was received from Governor Pettis, saying he would accept their services to the gallows. During this time the State had seceded, and the governor soon found it necessary to organize a vigilance committee, for the purpose of subduing the strong Union feeling then arising in that portion of the State.

The manner in which this committee was formed was as follows: The governor appointed the probate clerks of each county to act as presidents of the county committee, which consisted of twelve men; the probate clerks appointed five sub-presidents, to act in their respective districts, and take cognizance of all the acts and words of the people, and report the same to the president—probate clerk. The first proceeding of this committee was—under pretence that the Confederate Government needed all the arms in the county to be placed at the disposal of volunteers in the field—to issue an order for citizens to turn over, at the county-seat, all arms in their possession, which they would receive receipts for. A number, beside myself, refused to comply with the order. The committee then seized upon all the ammunition in the stores throughout the country.

Not long after this occurrence myself and thirteen others of my district were waited upon, by six of the vigilance committee, to learn our opinions, also why we did not comply with the order, and cited us to appear, on the following Friday, at the academy. This naturally caused considerable excitement. Some protested against going, while I advised them all to attend; and we did attend, with our firearms in our hands. When we arrived we found the president and his twelve men present, also the six who so kindly waited upon his. They announced to the president that we were there, and would answer for ourselves. We did not have any apprehension of danger, they all being our neighbours. The president then took his seat and requested us to state our views, and why we did not comply with the order.

My friends then requested me to speak for them, which I did, making a speech of nearly an hour's duration, in which I stated we did not comply because it was unconstitutional to disarm peaceable citizens, and that the order was not according to law, and did not originate from proper authority; also that it abjured the right and liberty of speech. We also protested that we had committed no offence against the laws, and that was not a proper tribunal if we had. I wound up by expressing my opinion in full, telling them that what I said was the sincere conviction of my heart; that their course would ruin themselves and their children, as well as mine; that we would be a ruined people—to which my friends added "Amen!" The committee then admonished us to desist from speaking against the Confederacy, and dismissed us, leaving us at liberty to return to our homes. Some three hundred persons were present during the examination, many of them armed, but all passed off quietly. I afterwards learned that some of the committee were very much dissatisfied with the result of the meeting, and allowed that the last d——d one of us ought to be hung.

Some two weeks after this one of my friends had business at the same town, and upon arriving there he learned that there was a company forming for the Confederate army. He was by some of said company assaulted and nearly beaten to death, and had to be carried home. This caused great excitement among the Union men, and many unguarded threats were made. Shortly after this the company in town were ordered to leave and rendezvous at West Point. The majority of them concluded that it would not be safe to leave behind them myself and friends, all of whom they threatened to hang, calling them d——d abolitionists.

On the night they meditated this diabolical act I was notified by our friends, and my old friend J. M. T——, who had received such a beating, came to my house to know what he should do. I will here mention that at this time no citizen could travel a short distance without a pass from the president of the committee of his district, and no one could travel a long distance without a pass from the probate clerk of the county, with the county seal affixed to it, and no man suspected of Union sentiments could obtain it. I told my friend I thought the best thing he could do was to leave the country; he answered that he could not travel without a pass. I told my wife to stand picket while we repaired to the house, when I forged him a pass and furnished him a letter, requesting him, if he should succeed in reaching the North, to have it published; I also gave him my overcoat and twenty dollars. He then left, and I have never heard any word of him since, neither has his family, who now reside in Illinois, (as at time of first publication).

The threats of hanging were now put in force; two of my best friends, more innocent than myself, were hung, but, thank God, I escaped. This naturally created great excitement, and some of the most resolute Union men expressed their opinion that now was their time—they must fight. We met and consulted together, but our condition was such that it was not deemed advisable to commence fighting. We possessed but few arms and a scant supply of ammunition, with no prospect of obtaining more in the country, and no means of communicating by telegraph or railroad with our friends abroad. We considered our case desperate. Up to this time the Union sentiment was very strong in that section of country. The news now came that a great Confederate victory was won in Virginia—the Battle of Manassas, or Bull Run. This caused a wonderful change of opinion. Union men felt dispirited, while the secessionists were inspired with a new energy, proclaiming that God was on their side, and victory must follow.

I am sorry to state that many professed Union men changed their politics and became sadly adulterated with the fire of secession. People were wild with excitement, and loudly proclaimed that every d——d Tory must be hung. A number of my nearest friends, who at one time flocked together beneath my banner, afterwards joined the Confederate army, to save themselves (they say) from disgrace or the hemp. They betrayed all our future premeditated plans. This sudden and almost indescribable change caused a great reaction. The Confederate authorities became less vigilant, and, through policy, they extended their hand to the Union man. You perceive, my friend you were on the wrong side. We can forgive you for thinking differently, but now you must be convinced that God is on our side. Our cause is a just and holy one, and we will soon gain our independence.

This kind of feeling was very prevalent, and hundreds who heretofore kept back, now boldly came forward and enrolled their names on the muster-roll. This change of feeling, particularly among some whom I considered firm in their resolve, so wounded my feelings that I became, for a while, a silent spectator, kept secluded at home, and had but little to say, though many of my friends would visit and try to persuade me to retract, to once more attend church, and take my old seat, where I had so often knelt and prayed God that the Union might be preserved.

I lost all hope of raising a force or maintaining the Union at home. In the meantime two companies had been raised for the Confederate cause, and I was offered a commission which would place me in command of either one. I rejected the offer, telling them that I would not, on any consideration, aid by any act of mine the bogus Confederacy. Even good Union men were afraid to speak to each other. Previous confidence was lost and every man doubted his neighbour.

Such was the state of affairs in August, 1861. At that time I had a heavy crop on hand to which I at once turned my attention, gathering and housing it. The country was flooded by the New York Day Book, published in New York City and supported by Southern capitalists. Persons who would not subscribe for it, no matter what their politics, it would be sent to them for six months *gratis*. Though I tried to remain at home, it was impossible, and, occasionally, I found myself mixed up in a crowd of people, listening to some fire eater expostulating on Southern rights, and filling the minds of the ignorant classes with falsehood and a desire for vengeance.

It was at one of these gatherings, in October, 1861, that my last and final difficulty at home occurred, which was as follows: One of my nearest neighbours, Mr. J. L. J., myself, and quite a number of others, were seated in a drug store, in the town of A——, when I asked one captain J. W. what he thought now about the war, and could he now look the people in the face, after telling them that he would be willing to drink all the blood that would be spilt in this war, and would support all the widows and orphans? how were matters now? If reports were correct there was an army of one hundred thousand men, on each side, arrayed against each other, and a great battle had been fought, at Manassas, and some six or seven thousand human beings were reported killed and wounded.

These remarks so inflamed my near neighbour, J. L. J., that, springing up from his seat, he said that no one but a d—n fool and coward would talk in that style. (He was considerable of a man and, at one time, noted for his fighting qualities.) This outburst of passion and insulting language fired me in an instant, and I told him there were those around who would testify that I was no coward, and for him to choose his weapons then and there. If he would not I said that he must take it back or fight me. This created quite a commotion among the bystanders and my friends flocked to me while his gathered on his side. Bowie knives and revolvers were freely and plentifully exhibited, and there was every appearance of a collision. His friends, however, advised him to take it back, which he did, and apologized, saying, that it was spoken in the heat of passion, and that he knew that I was no coward. This ended the difficulty for the present.

Mr. J. W. J. and J. W. were very wealthy planters, and had large families of children, and a long train of connections by marriage and intermarriage. They were so connected and so mixed up that they were sometimes puzzled to tell one from the other of these families of my district. The vigilance committee were largely represented. The news of the difficulty between myself and neighbour spread like lightning through the country, and the topic was that I had challenged J. L. J. (more familiarly called Bull Dog Jack) to fight a duel. This caused a bitter feeling among his friends against me, and they swore that I could not reside in that country—that I must die.

I had in my possession two double barrelled shot guns, which I loaded with buckshot and balls. They knew that I did not fear them, and were afraid to meet me on equal footing. I still continued to gather my crop, and, by this time, had forty bales of cotton put up, and twenty-five hundred bushels of corn housed. I should have previously mentioned that I had a brother who resided in my district. We did not agree on politics, nor did we quarrel. He belonged to the vigilance committee and had accepted a commission in one of the same companies that had been offered to me.

Meeting him one day he enquired what I intended to do, advising me to see those people who felt so bitter toward me and make up with them—that it was out of his power to assist me further. I told him that when it became so pressing that I could not live at home I should go North. He laughed and said that it was impossible for me to go North; that the lines were closed—blockaded—and that it was out of the question for me to procure a pass. (I, however, had no apologies to make, having acted on the side of justice and right.)

A few weeks after this, on returning home one evening, about

This is the spot and this is the tree.

dusk, and while in my stable lot, putting up my horse, I found myself surrounded by a body of armed men, who ordered me to surrender. I recognized among them a few members of the vigilance committee. They at once ordered me to accompany them to the town of A——, stating that I should there appear before the vigilance committee. I asked permission to go to the house, but no, I must go with them. After proceeding about half a mile, we came to a halt, when one of them remarked here was the place and there was the tree, and all the committee that was required was here.

This strange proceeding aroused my suspicions, and I said, gentlemen, this is not all the committee. One of them remarked that they would proceed to trial. I saw among them several. of my most bitter enemies and, in my own mind, decided that action rather than words would save me from their revengeful appetites. They now proceeded to go through a mock trial. They stated that many of those present were legal substitutes to fill the place of those of the committee that were absent. Here I was kind reader (imagine yourself in the same fix) without a single friend near me—my wife and family at home not even knowing where I was. Those were trying moments, for I could guess their purpose—actions spoke plainer than words—but my unbounded love for the Union, and my trust in God, made me bold and resolute. I did not fear them, yet I could not see any passage for escape.

After hitching their horses, they gathered around me and asked me if I would tell them the truth, and I answered that I would. The speaker of the party, in a very persuasive tone, then told me to tell the truth, as I had but a short time to live. I answered, I would, so far as I knew. The first question was, "Are you a Union man? "I told them that I was and always had been. Following this were a number of other questions, all of which I answered truthfully. One of them then spoke and said: "We have heard enough, bring the rope." Another then asked me if I did not want to pray, and I replied that I had not waited till that late hour to prepare my soul to meet its Maker. (I will here remark that two of the party were professors of religion.) I then asked the question, "What are you going to hang me for?" (By this time the rope had arrived but two of them said, "Hold on boys, wait a little longer"—at the same time gently pushing the rope back to prevent its being put around my neck.)

They replied, "for treason."

I asked, "For treason against what?"

They said against the Confederacy. I replied that I knew no such power, and neither did the balance of the world. The latter sentence aroused their anger. A portion of them rushed at me with the rope, shouting, with loud oaths, "Let us hang him, let us hang him."

I said "stand back, gentlemen, I want to speak."

Some of them desisted and said "Hold on, boys; don't be in a hurry; let us see what he has to say."

I then thought I saw a shadow of hope. My only salvation was to divide their opinions. I commenced by working on their sympathies—if they had any—but was interrupted by many questions. I tried to reason the case with them, but would occasionally use some expression that would arouse their anger, and again and again they would rush at me with the rope. Thus I continued: "Gentlemen, you say I have committed treason. All I have done is to speak my honest opinion, what I believe to be true. We differ in opinion and you are about to use physical force. You say you will hang me on this spot. Now, for instance, suppose I had one hundred armed men here tonight at my command, and you but twelve, and because my party and yours could not agree in politics, I should say, come boys, we are strong enough to hang them, let us do it. Is there any justice or reason in conduct like this?"

This seemed to have the desired effect, so far as abating their anger was concerned, particularly that of the two who professed religion. Then they asked me on which side I intended to fight, and I told them that I did not want to fight at all. At this one of them said, "There is no use of talking in that d—n way, we have all got to fight, and he who will not fight is against us." The same speaker continued, "Suppose Governor Pettis orders every man to turn out and take up arms and fight for their homes, then what will you do?" This was a pointed question and I knew not how to evade it.

I made the following comparison: "Suppose you tell me to knock down Mr. A. I tell you that I have nothing against Mr. A.; but you say that you shall knock him down, and if you do not I will knock you down. I will say knock away then, for I will be justifiable in knocking you." At this some of them remarked and construed the meaning of my language to be that I said I would knock down Governor Pettis, which was treason, and a great military offense, and swore they would hang me. They then rushed on me with the rope. I cried loudly, "Hold on, gentlemen, hold on; I want to speak; I want to reason with you." (Reader this was a tight place.) Through the influence of my religious friends, who cautioned them not to be in too much haste, but let him speak, they somewhat relented.

I then said, "gentlemen, you asked me to tell you the truth. I have done so, and for that you would hang me. Now there are hundreds in this county who are of the same opinion as I am, and if they all tell you the truth you will soon hang all the good honest men you have, and nothing will be left but a batch of liars and rascals. I have taken an oath to support the Union, this government, which every man has to do who holds either civil or military office, and he who violates it is guilty of perjury. Now I have said all I have to say. I am here and you can hang me or let me go."

As I thus concluded, one of the church members proposed the following: "Now, sir; suppose the Northern army should come down here and commence confiscating our negroes and other property, killing our children and ravishing our wives, would you fight them?" I replied, I would, most certainly. He continued, then why not fight them now? They have commenced at it already, both in Baltimore and St. Louis. I said, gentlemen, I do not believe it. We have no proof of it. He then addressed his comrades with "Come, boys, I believe Mr. ———, is perfectly honest in his opinion, only he thinks the wrong way—which is ignorance in him. He may yet change his mind, and I trust he will, for the sake of his family, and save them from disgrace.

This speech somewhat cooled their anger, and, with the exception of a few, they decided to let me escape, this time, but reminded me that I was not safe, by any means—that they intended to kill me for the insulting language used by me at the store—as previously mentioned. I then asked if they would give me any show. They replied, "Yes, all you can get," and, with this last remark, they mounted their horses and left me alone, and if ever there was a fervent thank God spoken it was then. A mind so much relieved, a heart feeling so glad, I bent my steps for home, where I soon arrived, my family little dreaming of the solemn ordeal through which I had just passed, and the narrow escape I had for my life.

I refrained from mentioning it to my family, for several days, and but little was said about it through the community, but I have reason to think that the party concerned felt really ashamed afterwards for what they had attempted, not from any pity for me, but because they had set out with the determination of hanging me and failed to do so.

Matters went along very quietly with me for a few weeks, when I was cautioned by a few friends to be on my guard—that four of my most bitter enemies were riding about, carrying their guns, watching for an opportunity to shoot me. My wife had become acquainted with these facts, and grieved herself nearly to death. Her mind was in a constant fear of my safety, both night and day. She believed, however, that I was governed by the right principles, which was a great consolation to me.

I now took my two double-barrelled shot-guns, and took to the woods. I had made some effort towards trading, and offered good chances for speculation, and my neighbours at once proclaimed that I wished to steal out and leave for the North, which caused a more vigilant watch to be kept over me. While living most of the time in the woods, I frequently saw my enemies, but not in any position to my advantage to attack them. They, in turn, would see me and would refrain from attack, on the same grounds.

Thus matters stood when I concluded to leave home. There was a few of my neighbours who had always remained true to me, and among them the following, who, upon learning that I was agoing to leave the country, decided to leave with me. It was in December when we started. I loaded up two bales of cotton and started a nephew—a young boy—with instructions to go to Grenada, and I would meet him there. I knew this stroke would draw the attention of my enemies, and while doing so I would be pursuing some other road.

On the second day after starting the cotton, myself, my wife's brother, and my cousin, with two others, met at my house, I furnishing the party with the necessary funds, and, at ten o'clock at night, in the month of December, eighteen hundred and sixty-one, we started, mounted. My wife's brother and cousin going one route, by the way of West Point, on the Mobile and Ohio railroad, and to join me at Corinth, while myself and friends would go by way of Grenada. (None of us had passes.) That night we made about forty miles, arriving in Grenada a few hours after the cotton, which I sold for six cents, bought some family groceries, and sent back to my family. The balance I invested in gold, paying two for one, also disposing of my mule.

When the hour arrived to leave Grenada, my two friends, seeing the great risk and almost impossibility to travel without the proper passes, concluded to return home, and, with sorrowful hearts, weeping like children, they left me. While looking around in Grenada I chanced to meet with an old acquaintance, who was not acquainted with my politics. He procured me a pass to Grand Junction. I then asked the commander of the post, Captain L. Lake, for a recommendation to travel on. He replied that I did not require one. I took the first train, and in due time arrived at Grand Junction. I at once repaired to a private boarding house, and kept myself as much secluded as possible. Citizens were closely watched and everyone was liable to arrest.

While here the news of the fall of Forts Henry and Donelson reached us, which gave me cause for much joy. Not long after this news I procured a pass for Corinth, through the influence of my landlord. On reaching Corinth I found many troops stationed there, and had some fears that I might be recognized by some of my acquaintances. I was disappointed in not meeting my brother-in-law and cousin.

After remaining a few days, I finally ventured into the provost marshal's office, and, after presenting my two passes, enquired if he thought it would be safe for a person to go up into Tennessee.

He asked, "What regiment do you belong to sir?"

I answered, "None sir."

Whereupon he replied, "It will be safe for you to go into the guardhouse," and instantly ordered me under guard and sent me there. I tried to make some explanation, but he would not listen, and I was marched off. Upon being ushered into the guard house, I found some two hundred citizens, and learned that the most of them were there on the same pretext as my own case, that of not belonging to any regiment and not desiring to join any, and were, in consequence, suspected of being Union men. Every morning we were offered an opportunity to volunteer, and many availed themselves of the opportunity, but I still protested. I had been here some ten days when the news arrived that the Yankees were coming up the Tennessee River.

After remaining in the guard house twenty-two days in all, I was taken out and brought before the provost marshal, who told me to go home, and furnished me a pass to travel south. The next day firing was heard at Pittsburg Landing, and the news came that Yankee gun boats had arrived and were shelling a small fort, which they succeeded in capturing that day. I still remained in Corinth, feeling secure with the provost marshal's pass.

In a few days General Bragg's army began to arrive from Pensacola. Troops were coming from all quarters, and great consternation prevailed, for it was known that the Yankees had possession of Pittsburg Landing. I had now fully resolved to try and reach the Federal lines. Previous to leaving home I had promised my wife that when I reached the last outpost I would write her a letter, and, in writing my name, if I made the Yankee lines, I would extend a straight dash out to the margin of the paper. If I did not I would give it a circle, which would indicate that my passage was blockaded. I felt quite confident, extended the dash, mailed my letter, and at seven o'clock, p. m., I started.

The distance from Corinth to Pittsburg Landing is twenty-one miles. At break of day I found myself three miles above the Landing, near the mouth of Lick Creek, and in the bottom, overflowing with water and full of drift wood, which I could neither wade through nor swim in. I had been fired at by Confederate sentinels four times but, thank God, escaped. After much perseverance I succeeded in wading and swimming across to the north side. I then followed the course of the river one and a half miles, when I was hailed by the picket and conducted to Colonel Davis' headquarters, where I had not been many moments when up rode General Sherman. I was then called to his attention, by the colonel, who told him that I had just arrived from Corinth. The general then ordered me to report to his headquarters, at the bluff, where I would find a double log cabin, and there to await his arrival. His quarters had not yet been established.

I had not long to wait before the general made his appearance, accompanied by Colonel McPherson, (the late lamented Maj.-Gen. McPherson. A braver heart and more noble mind was not to be found in the army.) I was then taken into a private room and closeted with the General and his Aids, when I was questioned closely, and answered all their questions honestly and truthfully. I stated to the general all my previous troubles, and, while so doing, could not avoid the shedding of tears. The general displayed much feeling and sympathy; told me not to be discouraged, that I was safe, and to make his headquarters my home. After being provided with food, I sat down to think over the past—my family at home—my own condition. I once more felt like a free man, while over my head was the flag, with its beautiful folds floating in the breeze, under which I had fought in Mexico, I there, on bended knees, sent up a prayer to our Father for my safe deliverance.

Troops kept constantly arriving, and in two weeks from that time headquarters were moved to the front, two and a half miles from the river, near Shiloh church. On many occasions I had been questioned and consulted by the general respecting the country with which I was familiar. He appeared to have implicit confidence in me, and allowed me many liberties not permitted a private soldier. It was he who gave me the name of Chickasaw, by which I am so well known in his army. Beside myself there was a Tennessean, by the name of McDonald, who resided between the Landing and Corinth. Mc. was a good Union man, but had to seek protection within our lines. He was very anxious to go and see his family, but the General would not give him a pass. I interceded for him and procured one for us both. I was to proceed as near Corinth as possible, and obtain all the information I could respecting the rebels, their designs, &c. This gave me an opportunity to send a letter to my family, through Mrs. McDonald.

We reported to the general next day, the reliable information that the rebels were in force at Monterey, and were advancing upon him. The general was not disposed to believe us, saying that the roads were in such a deplorable condition that it was impossible for an army to move.

It was on Tuesday before the battle that the general requested myself and McDonald to go out and obtain what information we could. At first I felt somewhat dubious about going, for I knew they were advancing. However, I started, and we succeeded, after making some narrow escapes, in returning, the next day, with the news that the whole Southern army was advancing upon him—as stated to us by Mrs. McDonald—that Generals Beauregard, Johnston, Breckinridge and Bragg's combined forces would, in a few days, pounce upon him and completely annihilate his army. It appeared to me that, upon communicating this news for the second time to the General, he still had his doubts. He acted quite unconcerned, and I could not perceive that any preparation was made to receive them, though some caution was observed.

At this time General U. S. Grant's headquarters were at Savannah, about fifteen miles below Pittsburg Landing. On Friday, General Sherman sent out a force of cavalry to reconnoitre. They returned with the information that the rebels were advancing. Another force was sent out that evening, and had proceeded but four miles when the enemy was discovered in force, and our cavalry made a hasty retreat under fire of a battery. This report fully convinced the general that the enemy was in force and nearby.

About this time an incident occurred which created considerable amusement at headquarters. About two miles from our pickets, in the direction of Corinth, resided a lady, who possessed considerable personal attractions, so much so that a gentleman belonging to the general's staff might have been seen to frequently ride in that direction. About four o'clock considerable stir and commotion could be perceived around the general's headquarters. Each and everyone's attention was directed toward the above mentioned gentleman, who came dashing into camp, apparently much excited, and minus his hat. His head and face being covered with a profusion of hair, resembling in colour a flaming torch, with eyes protruding to their full extent, gave him a ludicrous appearance, and he was greeted with a general roar of laughter.

After procuring sufficient breath, he stated that, while enjoying a social chat with the above mentioned lady, he was made aware of .the presence of a rebel force, and, with a hasty good bye, he mounted his trusty steed and, with lightning speed, he made for camp, hotly pursued by a score or more of rebels, who did not give up the chase until checked by the presence of our pickets.

The general had two clerks, S. L. Woodward find J. W. Bame, both young men, and gentlemen possessing considerable talent. They are now occupying worthy positions on the staffs of Generals Grierson and Dodge.

The next day was employed in drawing in the pickets and strengthening our lines. I asked the general if he did not think we were going to have a fight. He replied that we would soon have all the fighting we would want. I must here remark that, in my opinion, the general is a very extraordinary man, possessing some peculiar traits of character. An early riser—eating his breakfast before sunrise; of very temperate habits; seldom using profane language; a fine military appearance; plain in his attire; exercising his own judgment; governing his actions according to circumstances; approachable by all—the private can meet him with the assurance of receiving attention, and respect, as well as the officers, (though there were times when his temper was not mild.) I pronounce him a difficult man to read, but brave and good, possessing a high military talent, with a constitution adapted to the field.

An incident occurred, while camped within six miles of Corinth, in the timber, with no tents stretched. Upon rising, early one morning, he discovered one of his headquarters sentinels asleep. The general gently takes his carbine from him, and commences to walk the beat, which he continued to do until the sleepy sentinel awoke. You can picture his consternation when he saw who was walking his beat. The general approached and handed him the carbine, mildly telling him what a great military offense he had committed, and the penalty. He left him hoping he would never neglect his duty again.

Sunday morning brought with it an early attack by the enemy, rather sudden and unexpected. The general hastily mounts his horse, and leaves for the front just as a rebel battery of six guns is opened upon headquarters. The shot and shell were thrown with great precision, killing horses and mules, and ripping open the tents. It was my desire to accompany the general to the front, but, not having any horse or arms, I was ordered by him to remain and take care of headquarters. I succeeded in getting the wagons and some other articles away. In less than thirty minutes from the time the ball opened, the rebels were charging, three deep, and within forty yards of the general's tent. I thought it high time to evacuate, and made a hasty retreat for the river, with a salute of musketry in my rear—but, luckily, I escaped.

I will refrain from making any comment on this battle. Its proceedings have been placed before the public various times, by various writers. I will conclude it by saying that I acquitted myself with honour and credit, and was highly complimented by the general and staff. From this time forward I was treated with every respect by all who learned my character.

My next adventure was the storming of the Russell House, four miles north of Corinth, on the Purdy road. I volunteered my services, along with two companies of the Fifty-Fifth Illinois Infantry, and the Eighth Missouri Infantry, commanded by Brig.-Gen. Morgan L. Smith, who so gallantly led the assault. Some tall fighting was done, for about fifteen minutes, when our boys dislodged a whole brigade of rebels, and held possession of the place. Our loss was thirteen killed and twenty-eight wounded.

Nothing more of interest occurred concerning me until the evacuation of Corinth, two days previous to which I was present at a council of war, held at General Sherman's headquarters, near the Russell House. The following generals were present: Halleck, Grant, Sherman, Buell, Pope, Thomas, and others. A strong debate took place, and I distinctly remember that Generals Sherman, Pope and Thomas were in favour of immediately attacking the place. It was finally decided by General Halleck, commanding the forces, not to do so, and in two days afterward the evacuation of Corinth followed, by a safe retreat of Beauregard and his whole army. After this the army divided into three grand divisions, under Generals Sherman, Pope, and Buell.

General Sherman moved directly across the country to Shuwallah, situated nine miles due west from Corinth, on the Mississippi and Charleston Railroad; General Buell directed his course toward

21

the Tuscumbia Valley; General Pope moved directly south down the Mississippi and Ohio Railroad. I now inquired of General Sherman which way he was going, and he told me to Memphis. I then requested him to let me go and join General Pope, as I was anxious to move toward home, which thought was uppermost in my mind. The general appeared to be very unwilling to part with my services, but finally consented, and furnished me with a letter to General Pope, the contents of which I never knew. I set out on foot, and after travelling two days arrived at General Pope's headquarters, then stationed at Booneville, on the Mississippi and Ohio Railroad, twenty-five miles south of Corinth. I at once repaired to headquarters, and, without being introduced, walked into his tent and stood before him. He eyed me closely, with a look of contempt, and in a gruff tone said, "What do you want here?"

I made no reply, but at once handed him my letter from General Sherman. The treatment I was about to receive here did not look favourable to me just then, and I regretted leaving General Sherman. After reading my letter the general looked up at me, and in a very modified tone of voice asked me what I proposed to do. I told him I was willing to do anything in my power for the advancement of the Union cause, and that I desired to accompany his army into Mississippi, for there was my home. He dismissed me, saying in an hour and a half to report to him, and directed me to where his orderlies were quartered, to get something to eat, which I very much needed. At the appointed time I reported to the general. He then told me he wanted me to make a trip down South far enough to learn where Beauregard had stopped with his army, and to report the same to him as soon as possible.

This was a trying moment for me, remembering all the difficulties under which I left home, and knowing if caught in that country again my fate was certain death. I reminded the general of all this, upon which he said, "If all that General Sherman has said about you is true, then, sir, you are the man, and fully competent to perform the task." I at once consented, fully resolved to accomplish the undertaking, or die in the attempt. Two hours were given me to prepare myself and receive the necessary instructions. The general here provided me with a splendid horse and equipments, citizen's dress, and twenty-five dollars in specie. I started, but the day being so far advanced I went no further than the outpost, and remained all night with Colonel Haskell. At an early hour next morning the colonel escorted me outside his pickets, and left me with hearty good wishes for my success.

I was now alone in rebeldom. I shaped my course southwest, and was soon keeping company with fragments of the retreating army. They all appeared to be excited, and each one was looking out for himself, paying little attention to who was going north or south. After travelling this course some forty miles I turned south-east, striking the Mississippi and Ohio Railroad near Okolona. I there learned that Beauregard and Bragg had halted their army a few miles north of here, at a place called Tupelo. I remained here twenty-four hours, watching the trains and procuring all necessary information.

I then took a northeast course for thirty miles, when I stopped and put up for the night at my brother-in-law's, some six miles from Gunntown, in Itawamba County, Miss. I was somewhat surprised to find my brother-in-law here, who was to have met me at Corinth. He was dressed in the Confedarate uniform. I asked him what that meant. He replied that while trying to reach Corinth he was captured, and in order to save his neck he had volunteered. He had joined my brother's company. He said he was as good a Union man as ever, and had feigned sickness in order to be left behind and captured by the Yankees, whom he knew were coming. He expressed a wish to accompany me back, but not having a horse he finally backed out, and allowed he would go and see his family first.

I found it very difficult to travel north. Everyone wanted to know what my business was. After staying here twenty-four hours I shaped my course toward Booneville, through the woods. It was reported that the Federals had advanced to Gunntown, but I did not believe it, and so continued my course toward Booneville. Previous to taking my departure from my brother-in-law's I handed him a letter and some money to take to my family, in Chickasaw County. I had arrived to within about two miles of Baldwin, where I certainly expected to find our troops, but imagine my astonishment to see before me, and not more than two hundred yards distant, a Confederate picket. I at once wheeled my horse and shot into the woods on my right. They hallooed after me but did not fire.

I made quick time for a short distance, and felt quite satisfied there were no Union troops in that place. I pursued my journey, very cautiously striking the railroad again, two and a half miles north of Baldwin. I here inquired of an old lady if she had seen any of our cavalry that day. She replied she had, and that they were going toward Baldwin. I asked if she had seen any Yankees, and she said she had not, unless I was one, and she thought I was. I told her I felt satisfied that she had never seen any, for they had a horn and tail like a billy-goat, and wheeling my horse I put spurs, leaving her to her own reflections. I then made good time toward Boonville, meeting with no interruption until halted by the Federal pickets. They took me prisoner and carried me to General Oglesby's headquarters. It was then after night. I informed the general who I was, and he dismissed the guard and ordered his cook to prepare me some supper, after which he informed me that General Pope had moved his headquarters to Corinth, and that he was going there next day, and I should accompany him. The General furnished me with a blanket and a place in his tent.

I had been gone just six days, and had completely circumnavigated the Confederate army. I arrived at Clear Creek, near Corinth, where I found General Pope and reported. He expressed himself very much pleased with my services, and told me the horse and equipments were mine, which I felt very proud to own, it being the first present I had received from the Union army, and I began to have a better opinion of General Pope. I had not been in camp more than twelve hours when he sent for me.

On appearing before him he told me he wanted me to go to Columbus, Miss., and to start immediately, furnishing me with all necessary instructions, and promised that if I returned successfully he would make me a present of one hundred and fifty dollars. The money was no inducement to me, but I thought I could serve my country, and was willing to try. I started next morning, and about three o'clock in the afternoon reached Blackland, where I found a detachment of the Third Michigan Cavalry, commanded by Lieut.-Col. Minty. They had had an engagement that day near Baldwin, and a portion of them were then out. Just about sunset Colonel Minty put me through his pickets, and wishing me good luck left me alone.

I again launched out into rebeldom, taking a southwest course. After travelling some fifteen miles that night—it being very dark—I suddenly found myself halted, and two men emerged from the woods in my front; at the same time two came in my rear. They asked me if I was armed. I told them I was not. One of them asked, "Are you a citizen, or who in h—l are you?" I replied that I was a citizen, but did not belong to that settlement.

One of the party was about to ask me another question, when I interrupted him by saying, "Gentlemen, I hope I am among my friends."

One of them said, "Who in h——l do you call your friends?"

I answered, "I am a Southern man, and hope you are the same."

One of them, taking me by the hand, said, "We are, old hoss; but where in h——l have you been?"

I told them I had been up above, after a sick brother, who had been left when our forces evacuated Corinth, but did not succeed in getting him, for I found that the Yankees were too convenient, and that I was then hurrying away from them. I asked them to what command they belonged, and they told me to the Second Alabama Cavalry. I then wanted to know if I could remain with them all night. They said I had better get to the rear and stop at the next house, for they had been fighting that day with the d——d Yankees, and they believed that they would be along that road the next morning.

After leaving them I took a different road from the one they had directed me to take, and pursued a more westerly course. I travelled some ten miles further that night. I learned that the army had flanked out considerably since my last trip, and it required more caution. Next morning I took the road leading to Ellistown, but before reaching it learned that a cavalry force was stationed there. I then tried to circle it, by leaving it on my left, but unfortunately struck the outer picket west of town. They captured and sent me a prisoner into Ellistown, where we arrived about noon. I was put into a room, where I found several citizens, who had been picked up the day previous. The majority of them were soldiers who were returning to their commands.

The captain in charge told me we would all be sent to Colonel Chalmers' headquarters, which was about four miles southeast from there. Upon being brought before the colonel I stood back, allowing others to be heard, the better to frame my story. While standing there I was a silent listener to some of the most damnable falsehoods ever uttered by human tongue. Some of these soldiers, upon being questioned by the colonel, told him they had been left behind at Booneville and vicinity, sick and wounded, where many of their families resided; that when the Federals advanced they were concealed beneath beds, in old garrets and other places; that while in those positions they saw the d——d Yankees violate the persons of their wives and daughters, destroy their property, etc.

You can imagine my feelings, and God knows how I wanted to tell them they lied. And yet these stories were believed, and men shed tears, and swore by the Almighty God that they would have independence or death. It was such lies as these, in many instances, that so inflamed the Southern people against the North, and made demons of them.

I then related my story to the colonel concerning my sick brother, and he told me to proceed on my way home. I had not gone more than eight miles when I was again arrested and taken immediately before General Breckenridge, who was camped a little north of Pontotac. He questioned me very closely, and I related the same story. He also told me to go home. I then made a sympathetic appeal to the general for a pass, telling him that it was impossible for me to travel without one. He asked me for my County pass, and when I could not produce one he threatened to send me to General Bragg, who, of all men on earth, I dreaded most—for in his command were about four hundred men who knew me and threatened my life. I was then very willing to leave without the pass, which he permitted me to do.

It was now night, and, on reviewing my situation, I found that each time on being arrested I had been carried east, away from my intended route, until I found myself on the main road between my home and the main Confederate army. I felt some alarm about pursuing this road, fearing I would meet some of my old acquaintances. So I put up all night at a plantation, where I found five Confederate officers, with whom I entered into conversation, and listened attentively to their plans. I found matters quite different since my first trip. People were less excited and all were organizing and taking up arms, making ready for another great struggle. Every one throughout the country were ordered to report at places designated by the authorities.

Now that I was so near home, (within fifty-five miles, and nearly on my route to Columbus,) I fully resolved to visit it. Deeming it unsafe to pursue the main road, I travelled paths and byroads. Night overtook me within fifteen miles of home, near the head of the Yellow Bushy River. Some five miles further on I stopped at a house, to inquire about the roads, when who should I find in the proprietor but my own cousin. He recognized my voice and called me by name. He then asked me to alight, feed my horse and sup with him. He then told me he had that day been sworn into the Confederate army. After supper I took him one side and asked him not to make public my appearance in that country, for I had been wrongfully treated, and he promised me that he would not.

I then proceeded on my way home, arriving just before day. What was my astonishment to find my brother-in-law, whom I had parted with near Gunntown, on my first trip, and returning to the Federal lines. He had arrived a few hours before me, and delivered the money and letter. You can imagine the astonishment of my wife on seeing me, and my joy at being with them all again, and viewing the familiar spot where I had toiled for so many years.

My horse was sent to a place of safety, to be cared for by a friend, so as not to raise suspicion. I also sent for some of my old staunch Union friends to come and see me immediately. I found some of them wearing the Confederate uniform. My brother, who was commanding a company, and lived only half a mile from my place, was then home, gathering up stragglers belonging to his company. The following day, my cousin, with whom I had taken supper before reaching home, came over into my settlement and, in the presence of a number of citizens, announced my arrival. Notwithstanding my wife's joy at my unexpected appearance home, as soon as it was known that I was there, she became alarmed, and wept bitterly, fearing I would be assassinated.

My friends kept me well posted. The second night after my arrival, a friend called and told my wife that I would be hunted for the next day, by a pack of hounds, and that my brother would be with the party. I sent for my horse, fully resolved to leave immediately. At eleven o'clock that night I met my wife, in the middle of my plantation, and there, in the presence of Almighty God, we knelt together and prayed, and I believe it was heard by Him who "knoweth all things."

The next morning found me many miles from home, on my way toward Columbus. About noon that day, I met a young man who was out conscripting negroes, to work on the fortifications at Columbus, and from that time we travelled together, arriving at the place about three o'clock that afternoon, having travelled sixty miles in the last fifteen hours. I had no difficulty in getting into town, and did not part company with my young friend until after riding around and viewing all the works. After satisfying my curiosity I repaired to the Cady House, where a large concourse of Confederate officers were collected. That night they had a grand ball, while opposite the house was a large building which contained some six hundred prisoners—Federal soldiers and Union citizens. While the Confederates were dancing the prisoners were praying and singing patriotic songs. This occurred June 21st, 1862.

The next day I called on the provost marshal, where I found quite a crowd who, like myself, were applying for passes. I remained some time, watching and listening, the better to frame a story for myself. It required a voucher before a citizen could procure a pass to leave the city—of which I had none. Before presenting my case I was deeply interested, listening to the following conversation, between a colonel, commanding—if I remember aright—the Second Tennessee Infantry, who desired a pass to visit his wife, then residing in the vicinity of Tuscumbia valley. The provost marshal, Captain Gregory informed him that the Yankees were in the valley and would capture him if he went up there. The colonel replied, d—n the Yankees; he felt no alarm about being captured; he saw friends from there every day; that he would dress in citizen's clothes and go all among them, and find out what they were doing; and that his wife had some eighteen recruits for his regiment, and that he must go. He was granted a pass and left.

I now presented myself, and was asked who would vouch for me. I replied that I was a stranger in the place; that I lived in Chickasaw County, Mississippi; had come here with a friend, to drive some cattle, who had left the day before, without notifying me. He said how do I know whether you live in Chickasaw, or somewhere else. I then produced my papers, showing him my cotton bills of sale and receipts for taxes. He then propounded some hard questions. I convinced him that I was acquainted with all the prominent citizens in that section of country, and told him he must know we had hung all the Union men in our county. Upon this he gave me a pass to go to Chickasaw County—just where I did not wish to go at that time.

I had left the office and proceeded about sixty yards when I was halted and found myself a prisoner, and was conducted back to the provost marshal's office. I could not account for this proceeding, and, at first, thought that I had been recognized by some old acquaintance—in which case my life was not worth a cent. However, I did not show any signs of fear, but, with a bold, defiant look, confronted the captain, and, handing him my pass, demanded what he wanted. After looking me in the eye, for nearly a minute, he said "Go, d—n it, go; I believe you are all right." I felt much relieved, and, without further delay, procured my horse and left the city, on the north side. After passing the pickets, I bent my course east, and, that evening, struck the road leading from Columbus to Tuscumbia.

I had proceeded about thirty miles when I overtook the colonel, previously mentioned. He was seated in a buggy, dressed in full uniform. I entered into a conversation with him, and soon found that he had not recognized me while in the Provost Marshal's office. I was not long in working myself into his good graces, and, telling him that I, too, was on a visit to the valley, after a widowed sister, whose husband had fallen while gallantly fighting under Zollicoffer, at Mill Springs. I found but little difficulty while travelling with the colonel, as but few questions were asked me. When within about thirty miles of old Russelville, Alabama, I framed an excuse and left him. I had not proceeded far when, crossing one of the branches of Big Bear Creek, I was arrested by a Confederate picket.

From all appearances I began to think matters were going hard with me, one claiming my horse, and another my saddle. I felt very indignant, and demanded them to report me to their officers. I was then taken across the stream to a house nearby, where I saw some two or three officers. I then called for dinner, and requested that my horse might be fed. I saw the officers had no notion of letting me pursue my journey further. Just as we had finished dinner, up drove the colonel, whom I had left behind. He appeared rejoiced to see me, and our familiarity had the effect of changing the suspicions of the others, if any existed and I was not questioned any further, but at liberty to leave when I pleased. On calling for my horse, I discovered that my saddle was gone, and soon learned that one of the officers, a lieutenant, had taken a fancy to it, and stolen it, and sent me his saddle and a note, enclosing ten dollars, saying that he was well pleased and that I had better leave those diggings d—n quick.

Before leaving that place, in company with the colonel, we were told that we would not find any more Confederate cavalry on our course, but we would be liable to be gobbled up at any time by the d——d Yankees. After proceeding some two miles with the colonel, I framed an excuse and, pretending that my course lay in another direction, I left him, taking the direct road to Russelville, about twenty miles distant, which I learned was occupied by the Federals. In passing down the mountain into Russelville I met one of General Bragg's scouts, who informed me that he had to report that night to General Bragg, at Tupello, some sixty miles distant. (This was very early in the morning, and his horse was covered with foam.) He cautioned me how I was to proceed in the valley, as the Yankees were thicker than bees in June. I felt very much disappointed that I had no fire arms. I might have taken him prisoner.

I reached Russelville without any further detention, and found two companies of the Fourth Ohio Cavalry stationed there. I informed the captain that an attack was premeditated upon him in a few days, (which I had learned at the house where my saddle was stolen.) The attack did occur with some loss to our side. I requested the captain to send me immediately to Tuscumbia, which he did, under guard, arriving there the same evening, and reported to General Wood, commanding the post. The general knew nothing about me. I told him I could capture a rebel colonel that night, if he wished it done. He consented and ordered a lieutenant and twenty men to accompany me. I had, while conversing with the colonel, (my travelling companion) learned his destination. We started, and when within one half mile of the house, a charge was ordered by the lieutenant. The clattering of the horses hoofs over the hard gravel road could be heard twice that distance. This was poor policy, and it betrayed the ignorance of the lieutenant, who thought he knew it all.

Fortunately the colonel had not arrived. After the house had been thoroughly searched, the women making sport of us the while, they turned their attention toward me, and commenced cursing me, and allowed that it was a d——d lie, and they believed I was a d——d rebel too. My feelings were considerably wounded. I then told the lieutenant that if he would take my advice I would yet secure the colonel. After some considerable argument he consented. I then had him withdraw his men one half mile from the house, and dismount, six or eight proceed on foot back again, and so conceal ourselves near the house as to see any person who might approach. Everything being ready we had not long to wait before a buggy was seen to drive up to the house and stop.

Now was the time, and at a signal the men bounded forward and secured the colonel before he had time to get out. I remained concealed, so as not to let him see me, but at a distance I could perceive that he had shed his uniform and donned a citizen's dress. He expostulated, denying that he had anything to do with the Confederate army. We finally reached headquarters. He still protested that he was no colonel. The general approached me and asked me if I was certain that was the man. I told him I thought it was—that if I saw his face before the light I could tell, but I did not wish him to recognize me. The colonel still protested, until the general was inclined to doubt my word, and told me as much. I then told him, in order to convince him, that I was no humbug, and that I would confront the colonel.

I then came forward, and stepping before him and saluting him said, "Colonel, how are you?" This was a nailer; the colonel was dumbfounded, and you can well imagine his astonishment. He at once confessed, and turning towards me gave vent to his feelings by cursing me for all that was out, telling the general that I accompanied him from Columbus, that I was a d— -d rascal, and ought to be hung.

This proved a disastrous, a painful affair for me and mine. The colonel had learned my name and place of residence. In two months he was exchanged, and he immediately went to my county, and under the alien enemy act, entitled the "Sequestration Act," seized forty thousand dollars worth of property, leaving my family destitute. The next morning I was put on board, the train, and under guard sent to Corinth, to report to General Pope. On arriving at the latter place I was informed that General Pope was about to leave for Virginia. I had just time to see him and bid him goodbye. He told me to report to General Rosecrans, and he would make everything satisfactory with me. I then reported to General Rosecrans, whose headquarters were at Bear Spring. I had been absent just twelve days, having spent two at home.

I now appeared before the general, telling him who I was, where I had been, and who sent me. He took down all the items, and then said to me, "As I do not know you, sir, I will want some proof." This was a stunner. I thought of General Sherman, but he had gone to Memphis General Pope had left for Virginia. I told him that General McPherson knew me, and who was then in Corinth. He said he was going to Corinth that day, and taking down my proper name told me if General McPherson knew me that whatever he said would be all right. The general started, leaving me in charge of an orderly. He returned that evening, and early the next morning sent for me, telling me that General McPherson knew no such name, and that I must be an imposter.

I told him I knew that the general did not know me, and that I would go with him to the general. General Rosecrans then said that General McPherson knew one Chickasaw very well, and would vouch for anything he said. I told the general I was Chickasaw—that General Sherman had always called me by that name, but I hoped that I had lost it. The general then burst into a laugh, and said I must be the man, for I answered the description, and that should be my name. He then wrote me an order, and sent me to Captain Wm. Wiles, provost marshal at Corinth, for him to swear me into the United States' service as a scout, furnishing me the necessary papers. It was now about the last of June. For the following month I was kept almost constantly riding, guiding scouting parties here and there, until the army moved toward Iuka.

During this time an order had been issued to the effect that citizens who would report and take the amnesty oath would be permitted to bring in their cotton, for which they would be paid in gold. At that time the country was well settled around the town of Danville, and it was surprising to see them flock into Corinth and take the oath. There was one person around headquarters who was a cotton speculator, and who kept me, a considerable portion of my time, finding cotton. On one occasion two teams had been sent out, and were returning loaded with cotton, when about two miles west of Danville they were stopped in front of one H. L——'s house, where they were captured and wagon and cotton burned, and the mules and drivers taken south.

Sometime after we had arrived at Iuka one of the drivers, who had been captured, reported, having succeeded in making his escape. He said that Mr. H. L——, who professed to be a good Union man, was the person who burned the cotton, and told the guerrillas to be sure and have the Yankees killed, not to let them return. At this time our pickets stationed in that section of country were very much annoyed by being fired upon after night and several had been killed and wounded. This was then reported to General Rosecrans, who was then at Iuka, and sending for me, requested me to go to Danville, and by playing off sesech obtain all the information I could, particularly concerning this man H. L——. I selected six men, well armed and attired in citizen's dress. We started, arrived at Danville the same evening, and reported to the provost marshal, handing him a note from General Rosecrans, directing him to furnish me what assistance I required.

That same night I set out with six men and advanced to within four hundred yards of Mr. H. L——'s house. I then ordered my men to conceal themselves, while I called on Mr. L——, whom I found at home. At first he was very shy and questioned me closely, but I answered all his questions with apparent satisfaction to him. I told him I was a member of Colonel Faulkner's command, and that he had sent me here to learn what I could respecting the Yankees.

It was not long before he related to me all about the burning of the cotton, fully confirming the report of the driver. He also stated that he had planned and assisted, only a few nights previous, in shooting two of the Yankee pickets, and while his two sisters were preparing supper for me he wrote a letter to Colonel Faulkner, which I was to hand him. It contained the following statement: that all the citizens in that part of the country had taken the amnesty oath, not out of any pure motive, but for the purpose of selling their cotton, and that they all had arms, which they kept concealed, and if he would only come up in that country they would all flock to his support and help to clean out Danville.

I had now procured all the information I wanted, and bidding him goodnight we parted. I at once rejoined my men, and sent a portion of them to arrest him and take him to headquarters, which they did. The next day, as I accompanied him to Iuka, he at once recognized me, though I had taken the precaution to change my clothes, and begged me, for God's sake, to deal with him as easily as possible. He was duly examined, convicted, and sentenced to be shot, in five days from that time. In attempting to make his escape, on the third day of his confinement, he was shot dead by the guard. I felt sorry that I had any hand in this, still I honestly believe that he deserved his fate.

About this time hundreds of persecuted Union men were flocking into our lines from Alabama, Mississippi, and Tennessee, expressing a desire to fight the rebels. The general requested me to take charge of them and organize them into companies and regiments, and also to select such men as I chose for scouts, which I was to have full control of, and be his chief of scouts. Upon conversing with the refugees I learned that they wanted to become independent companies, and fight the rebels on their own hook. This the general would not permit. They then agreed to be sworn into the United States' service, if allowed to elect their own officers. This also the general objected to. They then became disgusted, and the majority of them disbanded and left, going in all directions. I think this was an oversight in our General. I am confident that, if granted the latter privilege, I could have raised a full brigade of good Union men, who would have been very valuable to the government, operating in that section of the country.

A few days previous to the evacuation of Iuka I was sent out to watch a female, who had been coming into the lines almost every day and procuring passes. After following her about four miles I concluded to flank out and come in ahead of her. I succeeded in doing so, and being dressed in Confederate uniform I pulled up at a house, where I found two ladies. I inquired if they had a pass issued that day in Iuka. At first they seemed to doubt my character, but after alluding to General Price's army, and telling them that I was direct from there, they felt better satisfied, cautioning me not to remain long, as I was in danger of being captured by the Yankees. They also informed me that General Price was then advancing to attack Iuka, and they were expecting a sister back from there.

At the same time, on looking up the road, she was discovered coming, with a Federal soldier by her side. This was unexpected, and I now must act; so keeping out of sight I waited until they came up, when I stepped out before the gentleman, with revolver presented, and demanded his surrender. He at once complied. The ladies then beseeched me not to kill him there—that they were placed in a very peculiar situation. I drew the soldier aside and managed to inform him who I was. At the same time, unperceived by us, another soldier, (Federal) who had been following his comrade, saw the proceedings, and managed to get behind the house, and was just in the act of drawing a bead on me when I detected him. Fortunately for me his comrade saw him at the same time, and motioned to him not to fire. He thought he had a good thing. This broke up any further conversation with the ladies, and we all returned to camp.

The information which I obtained respecting Price's movements was of much value, for at that time it was the impression of Grant and Rosecrans that he was advancing to attack Corinth. Another incident occurred a few days previous to leaving Iuka. The same old cotton buyer, previously mentioned, ordered me to take two of my men and go over to a certain house on Indian Creek, and there find a negro, who would show me where there were ten bales of cotton hid in the swamp. It was nearly dark when we arrived at the plantation. Riding into the middle of the cornfield we hitched our horses, fed them, and waited until dark before advancing to the house. At the proper time we started, and when near the house and still in the cornfield what was our surprise to see several men jump up and run like the old scratch. We retreated in an opposite direction at the same time.

After awhile we started again, coming from another direction, when the first thing we knew up they jumped again, "lickety scoot," while we turned, increasing our speed in another direction. Again we concluded to try our luck, but still we could not account for those men being there, nor could we tell what they were. We could see that they had arms, and also that they outnumbered us, yet there was no firing done on either side. Making a large circuit we felt confident of reaching the house this time, when the first thing we knew they were right before us, running away as if the very old boy was after them. We now concluded to wait until daylight, at which time we approached the house, without seeing our unknown friends.

Upon finding the negro he informed us that his master and three sons had returned from the army, and also a neighbour's son; that they dare not remain in the house for fear of the Yankees coming upon them; that they had been run to death all night by the sneaking cusses, but they had succeeded in getting away that morning and were gone.

While out one day, dressed in Confederate uniform, I met a healthy, robust looking young man, whom I concluded to conscript, telling him I thought he had been up here so long among the Yankees that he would soon spoil, and I would take him down to the army. I asked him if he knew where I could find some good horses. He replied that his aunt, living nearby, had three horses, but would not sell them to the Yankees. I let him go, not paying any further attention to him, and, returning to Iuka, reported. On the next the lady, and, if the horses would answer for cavalry purposes, to buy them. We started and had not been at the lady's more than one-half hour when I saw, passing the house, the same young man I conscripted the day before. He seemed to recognize me and hurried away.

The lady now insisted upon our remaining to dinner, which she appeared to be very slow in getting. In the meantime she had sent for the horses, when, the first thing I knew, the place was surrounded by our infantry. The sergeant commanding the squad appeared before me, pointing his bayonet to my breast, commanded me to surrender. Of course, I complied, not feeling the least alarmed, nor could I avoid laughing. Just then up came the horses, but, when I expressed a desire to examine them, they refused, saying that I would soon have other kinds of horses to examine. We were soon ordered to move forward. I told the old lady not to part with her horses, and that I would return for them.

In a little while we were carried before Colonel ——, commanding a detachment of an Ohio regiment then guarding trestle-work, some four miles from Iuka. He received me very coldly and, in a gruff voice, wanted to know who I was and where I belonged. I told him I was stationed at Iuka. At this moment I chanced to look around, and there stood the young man whom I had conscripted the day previous, with mouth wide open, grinning like an ape. Our eyes met, when, clapping his hands, he halloed out, "That's him; that's him;" and they all felt rejoiced to think that they had captured two secesh conscripting officers.

I now requested to speak privately to the colonel, who readily consented. I then told him he was very much mistaken respecting my character, and that if he would send me, under guard, to Iuka he would find me all right. I told him, further, that I would like to purchase the old lady's horses, and take along, as it would save me the trouble of returning again, and would be fulfilling the contract for which I was sent out. Thus the matter was satisfactorily arranged, and I paid the old lady eighty-five dollars, in greenbacks, for each horse.

I was taken direct to Iuka, and then to the provost marshal's office, who, on learning the facts, at once released me, telling the guard that they could return, and, if they ever saw me again around their camp, to treat me to the best they had. The boys left, looking as if badly sold. I now turned the horses over to Mr. Cotton buyer, who, in a few days, sold them to the government for one hundred and twenty-five dollars, each—a pretty neat, little speculation.

It was just after the above occurred that the general ordered me to take two of my scouts and go to Bay Springs, or below, and learn the whereabouts of Price, and his intentions. We proceeded afoot, keeping the woods and by-paths, avoiding the main roads, as much as possible, and travelling day and night. On arriving at Bay Springs we learned, from friends, that Price's whole force was then north of us, and shaping his course rather for Corinth or Iuka, and we turned right about, taking the most direct route through the woods for Iuka, striking the main road within twenty miles of the latter place, and crossing it between his cavalry and infantry. We travelled all night, reaching Iuka next morning, just in time to see the main column of our army leaving for Corinth.

The general was under the impression that Price was moving on that place. A small force was left at Iuka, under command of Colonel Murphy. We at once proceeded to Corinth and reported to General Rosecrans. Myself and scouts then had a chance to rest a few days, when the news came that Price had possession of Iuka. I was then ordered to distribute my men among the following commands, which were ordered to concentrate on the Tuscumbia road, east of Jacinto, Mississippi: Generals Hamilton, Stanley and Rosecrans, while General Grant would concentrate at Boonsville. On the morning of the day that the battle took place, a dispatch was received, at four o'clock, by General Rosecrans, from General Grant, ordering him to move immediately, and attack the enemy on the south side, precisely at four in the afternoon. This dispatch was carried by L. Bennet, one of my scouts.

A letter also accompanied the dispatch requesting General Rosecrans to have the following read at the head of his command: "A great victory won in the East, by General McClellan"—which was complied with. According to order, the general was on the ground at the appointed time, having marched that day eighteen miles—myself acting as guide for the general.

It is useless to comment on this battle, further than this that, for the number of men engaged, it was one of the most stubborn and hard fought battles of the war. The general displayed unquestionable generalship and bravery, and I shall never forget the noble charge made by Colonel Mower, and his brigade, while not a shot could be heard from General Grant, eight miles distant. Dark coming on ended the bloody strife, each army holding their ground. After the firing ceased, the general ordered me to assemble my scouts, and see who was the most competent to go to Iuka. On looking around I could not find a single man. I then proposed to go myself, and left immediately.

I parted from our pickets on the ridge, near two tall pines, and, after proceeding a few rods, found myself among the rebels. A number of dead and wounded were scattered around. The first one I saw was leaning against a tree, apparently suffering much pain. I asked him what command, regiment and company he belonged to, and also his name. My intention was to assume his, if occasion required, as I knew he would soon be out of the way. I had not proceeded one hundred yards further when I came upon the rebels laying down in line of battle. I passed to the rear, without being questioned—as a number of wounded and dead were being carried in that direction. I was now within one and a half miles of Iuka, on the main road which I found full of men travelling each way. I pushed on into the place, and learned that they were loading up everything, and preparing to retreat. I now turned my attention to getting back. I reached the tall pines without difficulty, and was about to pass by the picket when I was halted. They then asked me if I had any arms, and I told them they knew I never went without them. I was then ordered to give up my arms. I asked them by what authority they demanded my arms, and one replied by Confederate authority.

This was a stunner. I had not until this moment discovered the mistake, for while absent in Iuka our pickets had been driven from this post. You may well imagine my surprise, but presence of mind did not forsake me, and I replied no, never, and drew my revolver. In an instant, and before I could fire, I was thrown to the ground and my weapon wrested from me. I was then marched back into Iuka, and brought before the provost marshal. It was now two o'clock in the morning. After being questioned I was taken before General Price, who addressed me very kindly, and asked me what number of men we had. At first I was undecided what answer to make. I knew he was retreating-, and so I concluded that the bigger scare I could give him the better, and told him that no private could tell the strength of our army. He said for me to tell him what I knew.

I replied, "forty thousand."

"Why," said he, "You did not fight as if you had so many."

I said, "General you have been fighting only the advance brigade— the main column will be up in the morning."

He then asked me what force General Grant had, and I told him that I had not seen General Grant's army, but, from all I could learn, supposed he had more men than Rosecrans. He then asked me how many pieces of artillery we had, and I told him that I counted thirty-six, when we left Jacinto. He then asked me what I was doing with those clothes on, and I told him that I was the colonel's hostler, and he allowed me to dress as I pleased. He then sent for the lieutenant who captured me, to know under what circumstances I was captured. The lieutenant told him that I came to the picket post and claimed to be one of them, and when they tried to disarm me I told them that I would report them to General Rosecrans—which, at the time, created some laugh at my expense. The general then said he guessed I was out plundering the dead.

I replied, "No sir! You can search me." He sent me to the provost marshal, with orders for him to examine my person, which he did, but found nothing—for, fortunately I had thrown away my pocket book, containing papers which would have condemned me.

I was then sent to the guard house, and, at four o'clock in the morning, was started on the road toward Bay Springs Factory. The whole army was then on the retreat, as follows: Six regiments of infantry abreast, three of them on each side of the road, while the artillery and wagons kept the road. This manner of marching accounts for General Price's rapid movements—especially when on a retreat and I firmly believe that he can beat any general, Federal or Confederate, at that game. He marched this day thirty miles and camped near Bay Springs Factory. Just before night I was recognized, by an old acquaintance, as one of General Rosecrans' guides, and the captain in charge of prisoners—of whom there were about sixty—said that he would put me in irons.

Our guard consisted of two companies of the Sixth Missouri Infantry. I had now fully made up my mind to attempt my escape, the first opportunity. That night we were corralled on a side hill in the woods. The guards were placed around us every six paces. I laid down on the ground nearby where the captain was seated. The night was dark.

As I lay there, a major, belonging on General Price's staff, rode up to the captain and asked him what he thought the orders were, from General Van Dorn. The captain replied he did not know, when the major said that a despatch had been received from Van Dorn, that evening, for them to make a forced march to Baldwin, when the combined forces would attack Corinth, and capture it before the Yankees could return. The captain then swore like a trooper, saying that they had performed their part of the programme; that while they attacked Iuka, Van Dorn should have attacked Corinth; that he had a mind to break his sabre, and never draw another in the Confederate cause; that they had all the fighting and marching to do. I had had nothing to eat since leaving Jacinto, the morning before, and I asked the captain if we were not to have anything to eat. He said he was sorry to inform me that he had none for himself—that they had had no time to issue rations. I remarked to him, in a jovial way, that if he did not furnish me with some rations or whiskey, I would not remain with him. He replied, "Nary a whiskey." I then moved, carelessly, but cautiously, to the lower side of the prisoners, with nothing on but my shirt and pants, (the nights were somewhat chilly as it was September,) and I knew that I could not sleep much.

As the moon would rise about twelve o'clock, my best time was after that hour, as the rebels needed rest as well as myself. About twelve o'clock I awoke and, peeping cautiously around, discovered a sentinel, not more than twelve feet from me, and apparently very drowsy. I had previously surveyed the ground, and made up my mind how to proceed. The moment had now arrived for action. No one was astir. Gathering myself up, in a sitting position, I sprang forward, throwing my whole weight against the guard, clasping my arms around him and his gun, we both went staggering down the hill. I gave him no chance to recover his equilibrium. In the meantime, the other sentinels were aroused, but dare not fire, for fear of hitting their comrade—nor could they leave their posts, for the other prisoners needed watching.

After staggering in this manner, for about twelve paces, the sentinel fell to the ground, and at the same time I made one bound into a clump of bushes, where I lay sprawling at full length. At this moment two shots were fired toward me, but without effect. I did not stop until I had crawled about eighty yards. I then listened a few minutes, but could hear no one in pursuit—only some loud talking and swearing. In my scramble through the bushes I, unfortunately, crawled through one of those sinks so common around camps. The danger was not yet over, by any means, as the pickets had to be passed. After moving cautiously one-half mile, I discovered the picket, who I succeeded in eluding, by crawling on my hands and knees.

I now felt quite free again, and sat down to reflect, and study my course. The moon had risen, shedding a dim light. The stars were my compass and guide. The distance to Iuka was about thirty miles, in a north-easterly course; to Corinth about the same, in a north-westerly course. I then struck out, keeping the woods, striking across the country, going due north, wading through streams, across ravines, over hills and open fields. Just as the streaks of daylight began to appear, I heard the roosters crowing. This was a welcome sound, for I was so hungry that I had resolved to procure food, the first opportunity, at any risk. I approached the house, which was a double log cabin, cautiously. A bright fire was burning in the fire place, which showed very plain through the crevices and unplastered walls.

My only fear was that there were men around. "Liberty is sweet but hunger will make a man bold." The only weapon of defence in my possession was a short, stout stick, about two feet long. I entered the little gate, and was making for the house, when I was assailed by six or eight dogs, of all sizes and colours. They made a dive at me. I now had to act on the defence, and kept backing up to the fence, but dare not turn to spring over, the dogs were so savage. I then threw my stick with all my might; at the same time the door opened and a woman made her appearance, but the stick, bounding, struck the door, scaring the woman most to death. She screamed, slammed the door shut, and could not be persuaded to open it again.

I concluded best to leave. Still pursuing my course, passing through a cornfield I got some corn and water- melons, which somewhat appeased my appetite. At times I saw squads of rebel cavalry, from whom I kept hid—they were all going south. Toward evening I came to a large open field which I must cross. As I went, I increased my pace, until I was making about two-forty time. I reached the timber on the opposite side and, springing over the fence, jumped right on top of a man, who lay concealed in the grass and vines. This was quite unexpected. He did not say a word, but jumped up and put into the woods, and was gone in less time than it takes to tell it. I never learned who he was, or why he was hiding there, but concluded that he was trying to avoid the conscription.

About an hour before sunset, I perceived a lengthy column of troops, moving westward, and, approaching them very cautiously, soon discovered, to my joy, that it was General Rosecrans' army, moving to Jacinto, and by dusk, that evening, I was with the general, who expressed unbounded satisfaction at my safe return. After a good supper—food never tasted better—and some good brandy, I reported to the general what I had learned respecting the intentions of the enemy—their meditated attack upon Corinth.

The next morning the general ordered the branding of the horses belonging to the Seventh Illinois Cavalry, which caused considerable excitement in camp. The Seventh owned their horses and equipments, and this proceeding was in violation of the contract entered into by the government, at the time of their organization. This same day the general moved his headquarters to Corinth, and at once commenced to fortify the place, while I was ordered to send out my scouts on all the roads leading south, and to watch closely Price and Van Dora's movements—which I did.

Now follows the attack on Corinth, October 3rd, 1862. The enemy gained some little advantage the first day, but the second day was the hardest fighting, and in it I participated, doing efficient service on the general's staff, for which he mentioned his scout (without name) in his report, in the highest terms. I will here make some comment on the proceedings of this battle, which will not only interest the reader, but throw some light upon the high esteem in which I was held by the general.

While General Davy was being hard pressed on the Mississippi and Charleston railroad, the first day, I was ordered to go to General Stanley, commanding division to the south on Tuscumbia, and tell him to reinforce General Davy, with one brigade of infantry and one section of artillery, and for me to guide them, which was accomplished, and I entered into the engagement with them, and came near being killed by the explosion of a shell from the enemy. I then left this brigade, led by Colonel Mower, and, under a perfect shower of shot and shell, reported back to General Rosecrans that they were in position. On the second day, when the rebels made their grand assault— which was the most magnificent charge I ever witnessed, and seldom equalled—I was with the general and staff.

Adjutant General Clark was shot through the right lung, when sitting on his horse, immediately in front of me. Captain William Wiles, provost marshal, and myself carried him a short distance to the rear and laid him down, as we thought to die. The captain remained and I returned to where I had left the general, but he was not there, while. I found myself almost completely surrounded by rebels in their desperate charge. I managed to fall back, and at the same time our fort on the south of east of the town opened, and I never, in all my life, heard such screeching and whistling through the air. It was terrifying to listen to and witness.

Directly after I had left this position I perceived that the rebel line was checked, and, for a space of two minutes, they stood wavering, undecided, when the most precipitate retreat imaginable took place—every man for himself and the devil for the hindermost. I hurried as close in their rear as possible, without exposing myself to the deadly discharge of our own artillery, which was making sad havoc with their retreating and disordered ranks. On advancing some three hundred yards beyond where our lines were formed that morning I discovered several members of the Yates' sharpshooters, and among them a captain and orderly sergeant, both mortally wounded also the brave Lieut.-Col. Morsle, who called to me and requested me to hurry to the rear and procure some ambulances to convey his wounded to the hospital. I dismounted, leaving my horse with him, and started afoot.

On my way, I overtook a squad of rebels, and ordered them to surrender. At the same time, seeing a man trying to hide in a clump of bushes, I ordered him out, and recognized him as an old neighbour, then a captain in the Forty-First Mississippi Infantry. His name was Thomas Cookwood. I then returned with them into town.

Thus ended the Battle of Corinth. My scouts had all acquitted themselves honourably. The cavalry was in hot pursuit of the enemy. The general's body guard consisted of two companies of the Thirty-Sixth Illinois Cavalry, commanded by Captain Jenks, acting major.

During the last day of this battle a rather amusing incident occurred, which I cannot refrain from mentioning. A certain captain, who could be seen occasionally around headquarters, had, that morning, imbibed somewhat freely of the ardent what-do-you-call-it—commissary whiskey. Myself and an orderly locked him up in his room, thinking it the safest place for him, under the circumstances. This was before the fighting become general. After the battle ended I sought the room, with the intention of finding some "commissary."

I had forgotten all about the captain, when lo, there he lay, soundly sleeping locked fast in the arms of Morpheus.

After considerable shaking, he awoke. Rising up, he commenced rubbing his eyes. Advancing to the door he looked out, and the first object that met his eyes was a dead rebel, who lay within a few steps of the door. The captain looked, and rubbed his eyes again and again. Was it imagination or was it some evil spirit, that appeared in that shape to annoy him? Stepping out through the door, he turned to the rear of the building, when, behold! there lay another dead rebel. If was truly laughable to witness the astonishment pictured on his countenance. I shall never forget his look and the expression depicted on his countenance, after he became satisfied that it was no delusion of the brain. Looking at me, with eyes protruding to their utmost capacity, he exclaimed, "Who in hell has been killing all these men?" I then related to him the proceedings of the day, up to this time. Upon examining his room, it was discovered that some dozen balls had entered, passing through the weatherboards. The captain gave it up. He is no coward—which he afterwards proved by his bravery at the battle of Stone River, Tenn.

The next day cannonading was heard toward the west. I inquired of some prisoners what that meant. They replied, "They are getting h—l on the Hatchie." This became a by-word afterward among the command. I participated in the pursuit of the rebels as far as Ripley.

On our arrival at Ruckerville General Rosecrans received a dispatch from General Grant, stating that if he carried the pursuit further he would have to do it with his own command, and that he could send him no assistance. This left General Rosecrans at liberty to act according to his own judgment, and he decided to follow them to Vicksburg. On reaching Ripley another dispatch was received from General Grant, with positive orders for the pursuit to end, and for him to return to Corinth. While returning I succeeded, with eight of my scouts, in capturing eleven rebels near the Hatchie, whom we delivered over to the proper authorities.

Some time had elapsed after this when one John Logan, from Edgar County, Illinois, arrived, bringing with him a high recommendation, approved by several officials of his State, Governor Richard Yates' being one of the signatures. The general, after examining the document, sent John to me, to be enrolled as one of my scouts. I found John a truly patriotic man, with a great degree of self-conceit, confident that he could go anywhere in the Southern Confederacy that he took a notion to. I saw at once that John had but a very faint idea of the different characters he had to deal with. John was very eager and solicitous for a trip.

It was not long before an opportunity presented itself. A scout was needed to send to Grenada, Miss., and John was entrusted with the trip. After making the necessary preparations, and receiving instructions, he started. Some four or five days after this, while standing and looking towards the depot, who should I discover advancing on foot but John, At first I was in doubt whether it was him or not, he had changed so much in appearance, and was really such a sorrowful looking object—minus horse, firearms, and his good clothes; and from the manner in which he limped along I concluded that someone had taken a fancy to his boots, leaving him a pair that were a size too small. On presenting himself before me I was no longer in doubt that it was John, and extending my hand said, "Halloo, John, back from Grenada already?"

"Back from h—l?" replied John.

"Well, let us hear how you succeeded, John?"

"Wait till I get breath and something to eat, won't you?" I saw that John did not feel in the best of humour, and allowed him to depart. After his appetite was appeased, and he was somewhat rested, I took him into my tent, when he proceeded about as follows:

"After leaving Corinth I shaped my course toward Blackland, meeting some mounted rebels, who did not appear to take much notice of me, and I passed along, congratulating myself that I was all right. I had not proceeded much further when I was met by six more, who stopped me and commenced questioning me, after which they came to the conclusion that if I was not a spy I would make a good conscript, and ordered me to go with them. As we proceeded along they were very active in finding and chasing deserters and conscripts. Night coming on they entered the woods and camped. After building a fire and making preparations for rest the question arose, what was to be done with me?

"Two or three of the party declared they would not guard me, and another swore he would shoot me before he would guard me all night. Things began to look very dubious, and there was no chance of escape. I had been deprived of my arms, &c. At last they concluded to make me fast to a tree, and they proceeded to fasten my hands behind me with a grass rope, made me sit down with my back against a hickory sapling, and secured my arms to it. They then all laid down and went to sleep.

"After feeling satisfied that they slept soundly I commenced to work and twist, and in doing so wore the skin all off my wrists. At last I managed to raise my body up to a standing position, and while straining every nerve I twisted my head around so as to be able to gnaw the rope with my teeth, one of which became fast in it, and while in the effort to release it one of my feet slipped and I fell. I felt a sharp, quick pain for an instant, and discovered I was minus a tooth. The longer I knawed on the rope the larger it seemed to get; I succeeded, however, in freeing my arms from the tree, and crawled cautiously along on my body about one hundred yards. I listened, but all was quiet. I then succeeded in working my legs back, one at a time, thus bringing my arms before me, which was quite a relief. I soon had them untied. I then shaped my course, as I then supposed, toward Corinth. After travelling all night and the next day until evening I found myself back on the same identical spot where they had tied me. Of course the rebels were gone, but let me tell you I was badly scared. I then proceeded to a house, where a woman directed me the course to pursue, and here I am."

John thought he had travelled about seventy-five miles, when in fact he had not been more than twenty or thirty at most. I asked him why he did not go back, after releasing himself, secure their arms, and kill the last one of them. "Well," replied John, "I'll do it if ever I have the chance again, d—n me if I don't." I thought if John was not a better man he was a wiser one than before, and must have come to the conclusion that he could not travel where he pleased. I have since learned that he has rendered very efficient service to the government. When last I heard of him he had gone to Vicksburg.

About the time of the above occurrence General Bragg's army was in Tennessee, after General Buell, while General Price had fallen back twelve miles south of Holly Springs, and was very active in collecting forces and organizing. General Rosecrans sent for me and told me that it was necessary for him to know what Price and Bragg were doing, and asked me if I could ascertain. I told him I would try. So I resolved that myself and my best scout, L. Bennett, of Mississippi, would each make a trip, one to visit Price's and the other Bragg's army. I gave Bennett his choice, and he chose Bragg. We both started about the same time. I left my scouts in charge of Captain Cameron, provost marshal. I started on an old horse, with no arms, and taking pretty much the same route that John previously took, avoiding public roads as much as possible, made my way to Water Valley, north of Grenada, and south of Price's army. I there learned that Price was not able to act on the offensive, but was busy collecting conscripts, &c.

I now started back for Corinth, and found it very difficult to travel north. I procured a home-spun sack, in which I carried sufficient corn to feed my horse two days. On reaching the vicinity of Rocky Ford, on the Tallahatchie River, I was arrested by a squad of the Fourth Mississippi Cavalry, commanded by Colonel Gordon, in the following manner: upon riding up to them they stopped me, and asked me where I was going. I told them I was going to Corinth, and asked if there was not a place by that name somewhere about there. They said there was, and wanted to know what I was going there for. I replied that I was going to have some salt in that sack before I came back. They said they would put me in the army. I told them I did not care for that, but I must have some salt that I wouldn't fight without it. They told me if I went to Corinth the Yankees would get me and kill me. I told them I didn't care, I must have some salt, that my family could not live without salt, and that some of my old neighbours had been and got salt, and I knew I could, and if they would wait until I returned with my salt I would then fight as well as any of them.

It was quite amusing to hear the remarks made respecting me. Some of them allowed I was a d——d old fool, and they did not think it would pay to keep me, for I would leave the first chance I got and go after my salt—that I was of no account. They laughed at me considerable, and thought I was soft in the upper story. Finally they concluded to send me to Holly Springs, along with two other prisoners, guarded by four men. We went about twelve miles and camped. I had bought my sack full of sweet potatoes, which was all we had to eat. It was now night, and I sat up roasting sweet potatoes and talking about my salt. At last one of them wanted to know why in h—l I did not stop talking about that salt. At last they all lay down and went to sleep. I then got up and saddled my old horse, emptied my sack of potatoes on the ground, tied it on the saddle, mounted and started. Upon missing me in the morning my friends no doubt allowed I had gone after that salt.

About noon of the second day after this I reached Corinth, safe and sound, and in four days afterwards I was rejoiced to see my old friend Bennett, who had been conscripted, just south of Nashville, by Colonel Biffle, and carried to Mifflin, Tenn. After remaining a prisoner four days he succeeded in making his escape, and reached our lines with the necessary information.

At that time Iuka was considered neutral ground, and all the wounded of the two battles were placed in the hospitals there. A lady arrived from Missouri at this time and requested a pass through our lines, that she might go to Holly Springs to see her husband, who was wounded, also three surgeons, who were then attending the wounded belonging to General Price's army, and one Captain Bond, medical director on Price's staff. I was sent by General Rosecrans to Iuka, with instructions to proceed from there to Price's headquarters with this party, under a flag of truce, accompanied by four members of the Fourth U. S. Cavalry, (regulars.) Our conveyance consisted of one ambulance, the escort being mounted. Upon reaching Ripley we stopped to procure rest and food.

An incident occurred here which I cannot refrain from mentioning. On the west side of town resided a lady in a very fine house, at the time our forces occupied Ripley just after the Corinth fight. At that time she professed to be the strongest kind of a Union woman, so much so that General Rosecrans had ordered a guard to be placed around her house, to prevent anything being disturbed. And now comes the funny part. After alighting Captain Bond proposed to go over to Mrs. ——'s, saying she was an old friend of his. We started, and as we neared the house the lady spoken of was seen standing in the door, apparently eyeing us very closely. I had on a Federal uniform, and the doctor, previous to leaving Corinth, had purchased a suit of dark blue. We now halted at the gate, the lady still standing at the door, eyeing us with a look of silent contempt.

The captain thought it was time to say something, and calling her by name asked how her health was. Until then she had not recognized the captain, when with a few bounds she reached the gate, and clasping her arms around his neck exclaimed, "Why, Captain Bond, I did not know you with those clothes on; I thought you were one of those cussed Yankees." The doctor laughed heartily, while I bit my lips and could hardly contain myself. However, such is the fact, and there are many similar cases which might be recorded, and that the private soldier can testify to.

From here we proceeded to Lumkin's Mills, General Price's headquarters, and after being detained one day we were furnished a pass by the general and returned to Corinth. I had been absent twelve days, and on my return found that General Rosecrans had left to take command of the Army of the Cumberland, and left word that I was to follow.

General Hamilton was left in command of the forces. When I informed him that I wanted to join General Rosecrans he protested he could not spare me, but requested me to remain with him and keep charge of the scouts; that a combined movement of Generals Grant, Sherman, McPherson and himself, with their respective commands, was about to be made down into Mississippi, after old Price, and that my services as a guide were indispensable. Reader, that movement would lead me near my home, which I was anxious to see, so I consented, the general promising me good pay. The army soon took up its line of march for Grand Junction, where we were encamped for a few weeks, making preparations, during which time I took two or three trips south.

On one of these trips I learned that Colonel Faulkner would rendezvous at Ripley on a certain day. On reporting the same to the general he ordered me to report to Colonel Lee, commanding cavalry division, left wing of the Sixteenth Army Corps, the day before Faulkner would be at Ripley. According to orders I reported, and the cavalry moved out at eleven o'clock, a.m. That night we camped at the residence of the notorious Samuel Street, whom I expected to capture, but on reaching the house he was not to be found. At midnight we moved toward Ripley, fifteen miles distant, arriving there just at the dawn of day, entering the town from every direction at the same time.

Previous to entering the town I had learned that Colonel Faulkner had changed his programme, and instead of meeting his command at Ripley they were to meet at Hickory Flat. About an hour after sunrise we struck out for the Flat, and on reaching there we found a portion of them collected. They fired upon our advance, and then scattered in all directions. We captured several prisoners and their baggage, and returned to Ripley that night. Next day we returned to Grand Junction with over sixty prisoners, without the loss of a man. I then formed a very high opinion of Colonel Lee's military talent as a cavalry officer, and he has honestly won his star.

Not long after this the army moved down the Central Railroad. I was then ordered to report to General Lee, to act as his guide, keeping with him and taking part in all the skirmishing from Holly Springs to Coffeeville, where I received a slight wound. Previous to this, and while at Waterford, I was sent with a dispatch through to General Grant, then at Tullahoma, where I found the general, whom I had not seen since the capture of Corinth. The general manifested a warm feeling toward me, and I loved him as a father. The next day I reached Oxford and reported to General Hamilton, who had reached there with the infantry.

While resting here a few days I employed an old gentleman to make a trip down into Chickasaw County and visit my family. I provided him with a horse and equipments, two hundred dollars in Confederate money and fifty dollars in greenbacks. After being absent six days he returned with the information that my family had left, and no one could tell him where they had gone—that my property had all been confiscated. This was the first news I had received from home since my visit there while on my trip to Columbus, Miss. He also stated that they took him into a room and made him strip naked, and searched him, expecting to find some letter or papers from me to my family, but they found nothing. I received a dispatch from General Dodge, at Corinth, saying my wife and family were there, which was joyful news, although I could not tell what was their condition. I got permission from General Hamilton to go to Corinth, where I found my family in a good house, provided them by General Dodge. He had also loaned them fifty dollars and furnished them with rations, for which I shall ever feel grateful. After remaining in Corinth a week I moved my family to Memphis, where General Hamilton had established his headquarters.

The next day Bennett and myself thought we would take a ride out in the suburbs of the city and see what we could discover. We directed our course toward the south part of the city, and soon found ourselves on the Horn Lake road, and passed out into the country, without seeing any guard or picket, which I thought very strange. We met a lad riding a horse and asked him how far it was to the pickets, and how the crossing was at the Nonconnah. He asked me what pickets I meant, and I told him any that might be on the road. He again asked me where I wanted to go, and I told him we wanted to go down into the Confederacy, that this emancipation proclamation and free negro fighting had played out. He then called our attention to several houses nearby and told us that at certain ones, which he designated, we could procure anything we might want, but that the people living in certain other houses, which he pointed out, would betray us.

He also informed us that if we wished to cross the stream we would find a raft, just above where the bridge had been burned, upon which he had himself crossed the day previous, with the mail, and that we would find some of our pickets there who would guide us further. We then proceeded down the road, and after riding about a mile discovered some fresh wagon tracks, which led me to suppose that some smuggling was going on. We now increased our speed, thinking that we might overtake the wagons before they could reach the creek. As we came in sight of the creek, which was about three hundred yards in our advance, we discovered two men walking toward us, and on meeting them I asked if they had met any wagons. They answered they had just assisted them across the creek and up the opposite bank.

They then asked where we were going. I told them I did not wish to say where we were going, but they insisted upon knowing, and I told them we were going into the Southern Confederacy, in quest of friends, that the emancipation proclamation did not agree with our politics. As I concluded this speech I perceived that their countenances brightened up, and one of them remarked that it would not be safe for my friend to go down to the creek with blue pants on, but that I might go, and after stating my business to the pickets I could then return for my friend. I asked them where they were going, and one of them replied that he was going to Memphis to take the oath of allegiance, so that he might buy himself a revolver, after which he was coming back home to shoot a d———d Yankee for stealing his father's horse.

I then dismounted, and leaving my horse with my partner I proceeded on foot towards the creek. I carried a revolver, which I kept concealed from view. As I came up to the crossing I saw two men standing upon the raft, one an old and the other quite a young man. To all appearance neither of them carried fire-arms. I inquired if they could take two men and two horses across the river, and they replied that they could. I then told the old man that I wanted to find some Confederate soldier who would convey me into their lines without running any risk of being shot by our Confederate or any other forces. The old man, after a hearty laugh, introduced me to his companion as a sergeant belonging to Major Blye's battalion, and who, extending his hand, greeted me warmly. I asked him to walk with me upon the bank, to which request he consented.

After proceeding a short distance I drew my revolver, and presenting it at him ordered him to proceed at once to Memphis. A moment after my ear was startled by the sharp crack of a rifle, and at the same instant a ball whistled past my head, clipping my hair. I then ordered him to quicken his pace, and in a few moments we had come up

50

to my comrade, and mounting my horse I persuaded my prisoner to quicken his speed. Before reaching the city we overtook the two men whom we had previously met, and I at once arrested them both, which somewhat surprised them. One of them allowed that he was all right, anyhow.

Upon arriving in South Memphis, I dismounted and, turning my horse over to my partner, told him to take care of him. We were decidedly a rough-looking set of men. My comrade's revolver, and my own, were fully exposed to view, which fact was noticed by a citizen, who stood, a short distance off, a silent spectator. As it afterwards appeared, he came to the conclusion that we were a portion of some guerrilla band, and away he started, as I afterwards learned, to General Veitch's headquarters—who was then commanding the post—and reported his suspicions. The general at once ordered a squad of cavalry to proceed and arrest the last one of us, requesting the citizen to act as guide, and conduct the cavalry to where we might be found. In the meantime, I had started my prisoners toward General Hamilton's headquarters, to report to him.

On arriving at the general's headquarters, he had given me a note, directed to General Veitch, to whom I was to report. I at once started, with my prisoners, for General Veitch's headquarters. Arriving in due time, I reported to the general, handing him the note from General Hamilton. After reading it, he turned toward me and laughed very heartily, at the same time ordering me to bring in one prisoner at a time, in order that he might examine them separately. One of them stated to the general that he belonged to the Union army, telling the number of his regiment. At that moment a colonel announced himself, who at once recognized the prisoner as a member of his regiment, and, looking the man sternly in the face, asked him what in h—l he was doing with those clothes on. The colonel then told the general that the man had deserted his regiment some fifteen days previous. This man was put in irons, after which he confessed his guilt. The other two were sent inside of the fort.

Reader, about this time there was great dissatisfaction in our army, owing to the emancipation proclamation, and hundreds were deserting our cause, and horse stealing, robbery and murder were common occurrences in the City of Memphis at that time.

After the prisoners were disposed of, the general told me that he had sent out a squad of cavalry, who had found and arrested my partner, and, after examining him, and finding certain papers upon his person, he had ordered his release, and had sent him to act as guide to a squad of cavalry which he had ordered to proceed to the Nonconnah and destroy the ferry. The general then gave me my orders, which were to hunt up and arrest every d—n deserter from the Union army I could find, every horse thief and smuggler, and every citizen caught aiding deserters, or in any way violating the authority of the United States—and I assure you that Bennett and myself had our hands full for the following two months.

After arriving at home, that evening, I was glad to meet my friend, who had made a successful trip to the Nonconnah, destroying the ferry, &c. It had become necessary very frequently to go outside of the lines.

On one occasion, Bennett and myself were requested by the general to go down south of the Nonconnah, and, if possible, ascertain were Major Blye's command was camped. The next morning we started, on foot, and proceeded to the neighbourhood where we supposed he was camped. About three o'clock, in the afternoon, we found ourselves some fifteen miles from Memphis, seated on a log, in the timber, and near us was a small stream of running water. We had not been sitting more than ten minutes when we heard a rustling among the leaves. On looking to see whence it proceeded our sight was greeted by the presence of three Confederate soldiers, who were advancing toward us, each presenting a gun at us. Seeing that resistance was useless, they having the advantage of us, we delivered over our firearms, and were at once marched toward camp, which was about one mile and a half from where we then were.

After proceeding about a mile, and being some ten paces in advance of my partner, and guarded by two of the men, the third keeping company with Bennett, I had just crossed over a fence and advanced some six or eight paces, when I was startled by the report of firearms. On looking around I heard another report, and, at the same moment, one of the men at my side fell. I caught hold of the gunbarrel of the other man, who was just in the act of firing at Bennet, and commanded him to surrender which he did. After disarming them I found that one was shot in the back of the head and the other in the shoulder. The third person was now our prisoner, and we at once made him wheel right about, and, on double quick time, retraced our steps, arriving in Memphis, about midnight, safe and sound. We had learned all that was required respecting the camp, and, under the circumstances, had been quite as near as was desirable.

I have omitted to tell an incident which occurred during the first two weeks after our arrival at Memphis, from Corinth, which was as follows: Bennett and myself started out one morning, with the intention of proceeding to Nonconnah Creek, for the purpose of discovering the crossing of contraband traders. After following the course of the creek for the distance of seven miles, we discovered a party of rebels busily engaged in building a flatboat. After reconnoitring, we withdrew, unobserved, and decided not to attack them—they being too numerous—and retraced our steps toward town. On arriving in the suburbs, on the south side, we saw two gentlemen approaching us, mounted on very fine horses. When within about sixty yards observed one of them raise his hand to his mouth and, with his teeth, pull off his glove.

This act at one aroused my suspicions, and I told my comrade to take the opposite side of the road, which would, on meeting, place the gentlemen between us. Just as they came up, I drew my revolver and, in a resolute voice, ordered them to halt, which they did instantly— my partner also ordering his man at the same time. One of them turned very pale, and hesitated, which led me to think that he would either make an effort to escape by flight, or draw his revolver, upon which his hand then rested, but, luckily for him, he did not make the attempt. I then demanded of them who they were, and they replied citizens. I then asked if those were government horses they were riding, and they answered no. I then inquired their name, which they, hesitatingly, told me, also stating that they lived two miles from town. I knew better than that, and did not hesitate to tell them that it was a falsehood, for there were no such men living in that place. I then asked them if they had any arms, and one of them said no, while the other, with some hesitation said yes, he had a small repeater.

In the meantime my comrade stepped out into the centre of the road before them, at the same time keeping his revolver pointed toward them. I continued to ask questions, inquiring if they had any papers, and intimated that I thought they would make good soldiers, and I should be compelled to take them down into Mississippi, upon which one of them replied that he belonged to a command down in Mississippi, and was now at home on furlough. One of them produced a memorandum book, which I took, and the first thing that met my eyes was a discharge from the United States army. I then looked the man sternly in the face, asking him his name. He told me his name, and at the same time, I turned over another page of the book and saw it written in full, *Captain S——, Chief of Detectives.*

Without further questions I returned to him his book and told him to keep his revolver—that I thought he was all right. We then allowed them to proceed, which they were not slow to do, and, putting spurs to their steeds they were soon out of sight, thinking, undoubtedly, that they had made a narrow escape. However, I felt satisfied in my own mind that they were all right. The name and position occupied, as written in the book, convinced me. The name I did not pretend to see, betraying every sign of ignorance in regard to reading.

We now proceeded to our homes, tired and hungry, resolved to make a report the next morning of our trip. Next morning Bennett and myself left home and directed our steps toward the provost marshal's office, where I found Lieutenant Bryan, acting assistant provost marshal, with whom I was well acquainted. While reporting to him about the boat, &c., some person had approached me, from behind, and the first intimation he gave me was a light tap on the shoulder, at the same time announcing that I was the same d—n scoundrel who had arrested him the evening previous. The lieutenant then burst into a loud laugh, after which he told the gentleman that if I was the man who arrested him he did not wonder at it, for I would arrest the very devil himself if I should meet him.

The lieutenant then informed the gentleman that I was General Hamilton's Chief of Scouts. After this Captain S. treated me very kindly, invited me to his office, introduced me to several of his detectives, and told them that I was the cause of all the excitement, confusion and alarm in the last twenty-four hours. Until then I had not become acquainted with the particulars, which were really amusing. It appears that after the Captain and companion departed from us, they, with all speed, took a circular route into town, and at once deployed all the police force through the town, and several squads of cavalry were sent out, to hunt up and bring to his headquarters the persons of two desperadoes. I assure you I enjoyed the joke as well as the good brandy that was being freely offered and drank.

General Veitch had informed me that in all cases of emergency, where it required immediate action, and I needed assistance, in the shape of cavalry or provost guards, that the commanders of those detachments were instructed to furnish me the required force. The day after the above occurrence I was ordered to take a detachment of cavalry and proceed to the Nonconnah Creek and destroy the boat, which was successfully accomplished.

At this time it was impossible for a person to keep a horse or a mule, there were so many thieves in the place. My comrade, Bennett, had become intimate with a gang of them. On a certain night they were to make the attempt to steal the horses of Company A, Thirty-Sixth Illinois Cavalry. Bennett informed me of this fact, and I went and informed Captain Willis, commanding the company, who at once made disposition to arrest them. At ten o'clock that night his guard succeeded in arresting three of them, but not until they had unhitched six or eight horses. This horse thieving was only a specimen of what occurred nearly every day.

I will now relate an incident that occurred during the first week in March, 1863. The reader will understand that for two months Bennett and myself had been operating in the city and vicinity, running many narrow escapes from persons who knew us and against whose interests we were working. On one occasion I chanced to meet some Confederate soldiers, numbering fourteen, two of whom were lieutenants. I had been drinking quite freely with them, and professed to be as good a rebel as any of them. My intention was to arrest the whole of them, but, unfortunately, one of the party recognized me and it was soon whispered among them who and what I was. Soon one of the party approached me behind and, unperceived, struck me on the back of the head, which felled me to the floor, where I lay, insensible, for nearly two hours. Upon recovering my senses I found myself alone, every person having disappeared, and, strange to relate, until this day I have not seen one of them to recognize them.

My friend Bennett, when reporting these occurrences to General Veitch, had been fired at, by some unknown enemy, and narrowly escaped with his life, and the general very kindly advised me to leave the city, for a time, as my life was threatened, and I might be assassinated. Acting upon the general's advice, I was furnished transportation for myself and family to St. Louis, and, in the latter part of March, left for a more northerly clime, where I hoped to find friends. My wife was in very feeble health, produced by exposure to all kinds of weather, while stealing her way through the Confederacy into our lines. While on our trip to St. Louis, I had six hundred dollars stolen from me, leaving in my possession only forty dollars with which to locate my family, and that among strangers.

The loss of nearly all my money was a sad stroke upon my wife's feelings. Her health had grown worse, since our departure from Memphis, and, four days after our arrival at Girard, Illinois, my dearly beloved wife died, leaving six motherless children. Pen cannot describe a father's feelings at this sudden and unreplaceable loss. I felt as though my last earthly hope was gone. I was a stranger in a strange land, reduced to poverty. But who should care for my children? This thought inspired me with a new feeling, and I resolved to try and care for them, and, with the help of God, assist my country too. After remaining in the State of Illinois a short time, I left my children in charge of a widowed sister.

I will now refer to my old chum and friend Bennett, who left Memphis, shortly after I started for Illinois, for the purpose of bringing in his family, who were then residing in the interior of the State of Mississippi. On my return from Helena I found him, he had just returned and was unsuccessful in getting his family through. It was not long after my return from up the river when I received a telegraph despatch from General Dodge, then at Corinth, commanding left wing Sixteenth Army Corps, requesting me to come at once if not engaged. At first I was undecided, being at this time in the employment of General Veitch. I had also, some time previously to this, received the following letter which is a true copy—

Headquarters Fourteenth Army Corps,
Department Of The Cumberland,
Mufreesboro, Tenn., Feb. 15, 1863

Mr. ——.

Sir:—I am requested by Captain William M. Willis, Provost Marshal General to Maj.-Gen. W. S. Rosecrans to write to you, that he would like to have you come to this army on special service, if not particularly engaged. If you can come do so without further delay or writing. He remembers your scouting at and around Corinth.

Yours very truly,

John Fitch,

Provost Judge.

I soon decided to report myself at Corinth. Arriving at the latter place the next day and immediately reported myself to General Dodge, who requested me to take charge of his scouts. On seeing them I at first declined, they were not the kind of men for the business. I told the general if he had anything that myself or my friend Bennett could perform, that all he had to do was to command and we would undertake the job ourselves without the assistance of others. The general then told me that he wanted me to go down into the State of Mississippi and make arrangements so that he could receive from me papers every week—the *Mobile Register, Augusta Chronicle,* and *Memphis-Grenada-Jackson-Atlanta-Appeal.* Myself and Bennett started afoot, shaping our course south until we arrived into the interior of the State of Mississippi. I sent one man to Atlanta and one to Mobile, with instructions to take cognizance of the enemies' works, force and so forth, and procure the papers weekly.

Myself and Bennett were visiting the latter's family, the most of the time being spent in the woods, to avoid being seen, where we had our meals brought to us. While remaining in this vicinity, General Rhoddy's command was moving down from the Tuscombia valley to join Chalmer, Ferguson and Lee at Okolono, Miss., then to move on toward Memphis and strike the Memphis and Charleston railroad, between Corinth and La Grange. I immediately sent a courier through to General Dodge who gave him notice of this contemplated move, which resulted in a Union force meeting the enemy at the Tallahatchie, near Rocky Ford, and severely repulsing the enemy; the road was not injured. This was in June, 1863.

While yet remaining in that section of country an incident occurred of rather an amusing nature. I had learned that not more than eight miles from there was a gun shop which was repairing arms for Captain Warren, C. S. A., whose camp was about one mile from the shop. I at once decided to destroy it, and, accompanied by Bennett, started and succeeded in approaching to within one half mile of the shop. About one hour before sundown we had gained an elevated position so that we could perceive any movement made around the place. We discovered three cavalrymen, who remained until dark. After which time we concluded to advance and see if the cavalry had left; if there should be only three we felt confident we could overpower them if surprised.

After reconnoitring the premises closely, we could not see any signs of the cavalry. They had either left with their horses, or else had sent them away and were themselves in the house. I proceeded to the back door, which was wide open; my friend remaining in front, with a revolver in one hand and a shot gun in the other. I mounted the steps and saw a large mastiff standing in the open door, looking in at the darkies eating, who were gathered around a large table. I had not attracted the notice of the dog, and my mind was at once made up what to do. With one bound I landed behind the dog, at the same time allowing my foot to come in contact with his extremities, which had the desired effect of landing him under the table, where he commenced to growl, bark and bite.

My unexpected appearance so frightened the niggers that they scrambled in every direction, screaming murder, murder, upset the table, breaking the dishes, and adding to the noise and confusion still more. I did not stop to see what mischief I had done, but, opening a door on my right, found myself in the presence of an old gentleman, his lady and son, a young man belonging to the Confederate army, and, by order of Captain Warren was detailed at this place to repair arms. I immediately ordered them to surrender, which they did, without any hesitation, but with wonder and astonishment depicted on their faces. They could not imagine what this intrusion meant. I told them to remain quiet and I would not harm them. They allowed that they had done nothing that they were afraid of, and thought it strange that one of their own men should visit them in such a manner. I then ordered them outside the door, where my partner took charge of them, ordering them to take the position of soldiers.

I told them that Major Ham (Confederate army) was very much dissatisfied with them for trading and selling cotton to the Yankees, and that he had ordered me to come here and obtain the proceeds that they had received for it. Also to arrest them and seize upon all arms and ammunition they had about the premises. Also that Captain Warren was under arrest, and his command superseded by Major Ham. The old lady replied that the cotton she had taken to the Federal lines belonged to Captain Warren, and that she had paid the proceeds to him. I then permitted the old lady to enter the house, when she handed me three revolvers and one shot gun. We next proceeded to the shop, where we found nineteen muskets and shot guns, which I ordered the old gentleman and son to load themselves with, myself and Bennett taking the remainder.

We all, except the old lady, proceeded toward Captain Warner's camp, but, after travelling one-half mile, I concluded I had gone far enough in that direction, and the old gentleman and son desiring to return home for some blankets, I permitted them to do so, after they had pledged their word to report to Major Ham's camp, at seven o'clock next morning. We were now alone, and at once left the road, crossing a cornfield, until we reached a low bottom land, where we buried the guns in the mud—and there they undoubtedly remain until this day. From this place we made all haste back to our old section, and, the next day, sent an old man down into the vicinity of the gunsmith's, to ascertain what effect our visit had produced.

The old gentleman returned, in due time, and stated that the father and son had reported at camp, according to promise, but found Captain Warren still in command, and that he knew nothing about my Major Ham, and told the grieved party that they had been badly fooled by two d——n homemade Yankees.

In the meantime, my newspapers, for which I had subscribed and paid for six months, had arrived at the post office, and my friends had arrived from Mobile and Atlanta, and all intermediate points, bringing all the necessary information. I now established a line of couriers, to ply between the post office and to within fifteen miles of Corinth. I also had plenty of Confederate money, having captured the Sheriff and County Treasurer of Franklin County, Alabama, who had in their possession fourteen thousand dollars. I expended this money freely among my scouts and couriers. The reader can perceive by this that there must have been good Union men residing in the South, without whose assistance many of my plans would have proved failures. While laying out in the woods, waiting for my scouts to report, my meals were brought to me by a young lady, and I promised that, if she would come to Corinth, her services would be rewarded.

I now had everything arranged to my satisfaction, and left for Corinth, which was sixty miles north, travelling all the way through the woods afoot, arriving on the second day of July, making the trip in forty hours, and reported to the general who was much pleased. He again requested me to take charge of his scouts, numbering fifteen, and to increase them to twenty-five, which I did. About one half of them were citizens, who were residing in the county, and the other half soldiers detailed from the ranks. My next plan was to establish three more lines of couriers, in different directions, whose business was outside the lines, not to come unless ordered to do so. I have every reason to believe that General Dodge, at this time, had better facilities for being posted than any other general in the Union army.

In the meantime, the young lady I have previously spoken of, made her appearance in Corinth. I knew of no better way to remunerate her than to offer her my heart and hand, which she, at once accepted—God bless her—and has, so far, proved a good, faithful wife and stepmother. An amusing incident occurred on the day of my marriage. Some of the boys came to the little frame house I was then living in, and, without waiting to see me, called out that Colonel Mercer, then commanding the post, in the absence of General Dodge, required me to saddle my horse immediately. I learned the boys were trying to play off a joke on me.

About ten o'clock, that same night, an orderly came with the same message, but I paid no attention to it. Not long after this another came, knocking at the door. This annoyance began to bore me considerably, and I jumped out of bed and opened the door, expecting to see the fellow, but he did not wait, and I could not see who it was. I called after him, "Tell the colonel to go to h—l." I had hardly got in bed before another *rap, rap, rap*, came, on the door, and a voice calling me said that the colonel wanted me to come right away—and if I did not I had better. I at once opened the door and, sure enough, there stood the colonel's orderly.

This was no joke. I was soon dressed, and reported myself to Colonel Mercer, who I found not in the best of humour, and, in broken English, he wanted to know, "Vat for, py God, you no report yourself to me, when I sends vor you? Ah, py God, and you keep me waiting all de hole night, py God. I sens my orderly some two, three times, and you no comes, py tarn. I no like dis, and I vants to know de vy you tells mine orderly to say to me go to h—l, eh? Vat for you say dis? Ah, py God"—and thus he continued for some time.

At last he told me he wanted a guide to send out with a scouting party, which order I filled in a few minutes. The next day I called on the colonel, and explained to him why it was that I did not obey his orderly—that the boys had been plaguing me because I had only that day got married. This was a proceeding the colonel had known nothing about, and when I finished he said, "So you gets married, eh? Veil, dat ish goot. I forgives you dis time, and hopes you have lots of little poys. Now we takes a drink of brandy. So good day"—and I left the colonel in the best of spirits.

My position was of such a nature, at this time, that I had but little chance to participate in many of the scouts or raids, made into the enemy's country. Having twenty-five men under my immediate command and control, subject to no orders, except what came from myself; (I was at liberty to discharge and employ my men;) keeping my own books, without the help of a clerk or orderly; attending to the wants of my company for commissary and quartermaster stores, ordnance, camp and garrison equipage; making out of pay rolls, and receiving funds for paying my men—no one of whom got less than one hundred dollars a month; kept me constantly employed. I would have as many as eight scouts out at a time, operating in various directions, and be receiving reports daily, which had to be handed in at headquarters by myself. When I did absent myself I appointed a suitable man to conduct the business. I felt proud of my position, and my commanding officer, Brig.-Gen., since Maj.-Gen. Dodge, one of the bravest of the brave, was one who could appreciate valuable services, when rendered.

Twice a week I had to send scouts to communicate with the gunboats at Pittsburg Landing, twenty-one miles north. On the other hand, I had to have scouts out whose business it was to communicate with my outside cousins, fifteen miles from Corinth, bringing in the Southern papers, which kept about one-half of my men out all the time. In this way was business conducted most successfully, from July 1st, 1863 until November of the same year. Not unfrequently during this time have I taken ten or a dozen men, when learning of some rebel rendezvous, and surprised the enemy in their camp, and almost invariably with success. I must omit giving attention to a hundred or more incidents which occurred while scouting—they are too numerous to mention, and would occupy too much space. I will relate a few of the most startling and interesting ones.

About the last of July, having learned that a party of guerrillas and bushwhackers were making their headquarters at a certain house on Brown's Creek, some thirty miles south of Corinth, near Bay Springs, I resolved to capture them, although I could only take six of my men, the most of them being absent on duty. One morning, just as daylight began to appear, we started, riding all day, and arriving at the vicinity of our destination about four o'clock. After reconnoitring and satisfying ourselves as to their position, we charged their camp. It was a complete surprise, we, however, captured but two prisoners, and five horses—the rest being absent on a scout. We destroyed their camp and garrison equipage. It was now near sundown, and we learned, from reliable sources, that not more than two miles distant, there were camped some twenty-five Confederate Cavalry, who had only come into that section of country the day previous.

After talking the matter over, we came to the conclusion that we would retrace our steps toward home, taking the two prisoners along, and also a few extra horses, our own being tired and hungry. We must also procure corn for them before dark. After reaching the Tuscumbia and Fulton road, we crossed a bridge and turned into the woods, proceeded about four hundred yards and, dismounting, unsaddled and fed our horses, intending to remain at that place until midnight. Our arms, on this occasion, consisted of three double-barrelled shot-guns and three fine shooting rifles, and two navy revolvers, each. Feeling confident that we would be pursued, I determined to fight them in their own style that night.

After waiting about one hour we prepared for action. Leaving one man to guard the two prisoners and all the horses, with instructions if either of the prisoners tried to escape or made a noise to shoot him on the spot, we started for the main road. On reaching it, we selected a favourable position and laid down. We had not been waiting long when we heard the enemy approaching, as they crossed the bridge. Judging from the noise they made in crossing it, we supposed there were about fifteen of them. As they advanced to within about forty yards I halted them. They obeyed instantly. I then asked them to what command they belonged, and they answered to Major Ham's, at the same time inquiring to what one we belonged. I answered Rhoddy's, and, in the same breath, gave the word to my men to fire, which they did, pouring in a volley that somewhat disturbed the stillness of the night, and created a complete stampede of men and horses—some turning into the timber and others recrossing the bridge.

All soon became quiet again, with the exception of a loose horse, stumbling over the fallen timber, and the groans of the wounded. Without changing our position, we reloaded our guns, and had been waiting about half an hour when several were seen to approach' again, from the same direction. Halting at a more respectful distance they commenced to call loudly, and the following dialogue ensued:

"Halloo, there."

"Halloo."

"What in h—l do you mean ?"

"You don't come that on me. You are the d—n Feds that went down the road this morning."

"No, by God, we are Rebels, and belong to Major Ham's command. You must be d—n fools."

"If you are Confederates, three of you advance."

(Three of them advanced to where they had been fired into and halted.)

"Dismount, and advance afoot."

"No, that is not right."

"I believe you are the d—n Yankees who went down the road this morning."

"No sir, we are pursuing them. They captured two of our men, this evening, five miles from here."

"Advance."

"No, one of you advance."

At this, I ordered the boys to let them have it, and we all blazed away—which caused another stampede. Very soon all became quiet again. The night was intensely dark. We again reloaded our guns, and all was ready. My attention was now attracted by a noise in the bush, on our left, which impressed me with the idea that a flank movement was going on. At the same time a voice was heard, coming from the direction of the bridge, to which I paid no attention. One of our men remarked that he would go and see what that groaning meant in our front. He had no sooner said it than a volley was poured into us from our left, which made things rattle around us. We instantly returned the fire, and a general fight ensued.

Emptying our guns and revolvers, we silenced the enemy, and then began to fall back slowly, for about sixty yards, when we again took a position and loaded our guns and revolvers. Remaining quiet, we could now hear them coming out of the bush into the road, near the same spot we had left. One of them remarked that he reckoned they had given us h—l; to look sharp for he believed they must have killed some of us. At this I told the boys to let them have it, and away went another volley—and away went the rebels. We could not hear or see any more of them that night, and, returning to our horses, found our prisoners all right.

It being now midnight, we saddled up, mounted and started, arriving in Corinth the next morning. A few days after this occurrence, we captured two of Major Ham's men. Upon questioning them about General Rhoddy's men, they replied, d—n Rhoddy's men; that they had had a fight with them the other night, and that two of their men had been killed and three wounded and five horses killed; that they were a set of d—n fools. This news pleased me very much and I did not dispute it.

About this time, there was a band of guerrillas, commanded by one Dr. Smith, who operated between Corinth and the Tennessee River. They became a terror to the Union inhabitants of that vicinity. The leader was a brave and desperate man. My instructions from the General were to break up the band, if possible. They had captured two of my scouts, while they were bearing dispatches to the Tennessee River, one of whom escaped, but the other I have never heard from since. I now selected seven of my men, and, all being well armed, we started out, mounted, for their rendezvous, determined to give them battle, at all hazards, if found.

After proceeding about fourteen miles, on the Hamburg road, we halted, dismounted, and, after concealing our horses, took up a position at a cross-road, where we remained all night, expecting them to pass that way. As they did their travelling in the night, and morning came without the guerrillas making their appearance, we mounted our horses and rode about a mile to a plantation, where we procured breakfast. We had just concluded our meal, and the order had been given to prepare to mount, when we discovered Dr. Smith, and seventeen of his men, advancing, following our trail. My men fell into line as quickly as possible, while shots were being rapidly exchanged from both sides, at not more than two hundred yards.

Dr. Smith, leading his men, ordered them to charge. I now had my men in line, and ordered them to charge, both parties firing and yelling like Indians. This movement was rather unexpected by them, and was made with so much determination, that they broke and fled in all directions, leaving on the field two men wounded—one of them mortally, and we also captured five guns. I had one man wounded, but not seriously. After caring for the wounded, we started for Corinth, but not by the direct road, which, had we taken, would have proved fatal to us—as I afterward learned that Dr. Smith rallied ten of his men and took a position on the direct road to Corinth, expecting us to pass that way. Neither party was satisfied with the result of this fight, and Smith was still at large.

It was now my intention to start out with a larger force and pursue Smith to the death; but before I was ready to start the Seventh Illinois mounted infantry, Colonel Rowett, commanding, while on a scout had come unexpectedly upon Smith's band and completely broken it up, Smith narrowly escaping. He left the country for other parts.

Myself and six of my men started out mounted, all dressed in Confederate uniform and armed to the teeth, directing our course toward Fulton, Miss. After riding three days, and finding nothing of any importance, we concluded to return home. When within about twenty miles of Corinth we stopped at the plantation of a very wealthy secessionist, where we procured supper, the inmates extending every courtesy, under the impression that we were good Southern men. While at supper a lady made her appearance, having just arrived from a neighbouring house, to inquire to what command we belonged. I asked her why she wished to know, and she replied that there were twelve of Major Ham's command up at her house, getting supper, who wished to know.

I told her we belonged to Captain Davenport's command (rebel.) Just as we were about ready to start an old gentleman made his appearance, coming from the same house, and inquired which way we were travelling, and what we were doing in that section. I told him to tell Major Ham's men that we would be up there in a few minutes to see them. "We were soon ready and mounted, and as we approached the next house, which was by the roadside, we discovered a company of men mounted and drawn up in line, with their guns ready for instant use. The moon was shining brightly, and as we rode up to within a few yards of them the captain commanding inquired which way we were going. I replied that we were skylarking around, to see what we could find, and that we expected to go up into the valley. I then asked them what they were doing there. He replied that they were sent out to watch the roads, and learn what they could about the Yankees, but as yet he had learned nothing.

One of my men now proposed to swap horses, but could not agree, so we proceeded on our way, thinking it would not pay to attack them under the circumstances. They were in doubt as to our character. We arrived safely at Corinth, without meeting with any further incident.

Another incident occurred which is quite amusing to think of, though anything but profitable to us at the time. We had learned that at a wealthy old rebel's plantation, about forty miles south of Corinth, there were some very fine horses, and as our stock needed replenishing I concluded to take a few of my men and capture them. I selected B. and H., and we started, arriving in due time at the plantation. We concealed ourselves in the woods until night, when we proceeded toward the house. B. went to reconnoitre, and shortly returned, stating that a very fine stallion and two blooded mares were in the stable lot. We concluded to wait until the inmates of the house should retire before attempting to catch the stock.

After waiting as we thought a sufficient length of time we started for the lot. The night was dark, and we did not discover, until close by, that the lot was full of horses, and at the same time we heard men talking and laughing. B. and H. started into the stable, while I kept concealed in a shed. Just then a number of men entered the lot and commenced catching their horses, saddling up, and preparing to start. This was unexpected company, and we were in doubt as to their number. I told the boys to hide, if possible, but if discovered to let into them, and we would get out the best we could. The newcomers began to show themselves in every quarter, but I had a very indistinct view of them as they passed close by me, trying to catch their horses. I was then lying flat on my back, close in the panels of the fence, and B. and H. were cooped up in the stable, under the mangers.

It was not long before the horses were all secured and saddled, and nine men were seen to mount and ride off, followed by a negro, riding one and leading two, the same that we had come so far to procure. We now retraced our steps toward home, arriving there without meeting with any accident. While passing through a swamp two armed rebels rode up to us, and in a very rough manner demanded what we were doing there, and where we were going; they were under the impression that we were deserters from the rebel army. After parleying a few minutes I drew my navy revolver—which I carried concealed beneath my coat—and told them they were prisoners, and must accompany us. We brought them into Corinth, not meeting with any further trouble, but feeling very cheap over our disappointment in not getting the horses.

About this time General Rhoddy had his command scattered along Bear Creek, guarding all points where it was possible for any force to cross. Several attempts had been made to send scouts up into the valley. General Dodge told me it was highly necessary that he should obtain some reliable information from that quarter. I at once concluded to make the effort, and taking six of my men we started. After dark we arrived at the plantation of a doctor, with whom I had formerly been acquainted, and thought to be a good Union man, he having taken the oath of allegiance at the time our forces occupied Iuka. When within half a mile of his house we turned into the timber, where I left all my men except one, who accompanied me to the house, leaving our horses behind.

On arriving at the house we found that the inmates had all retired to rest, but we at once aroused them, and they got up and went to work preparing us a supper. The old doctor did not recognize me in my Confederate uniform. They seemed to feel glad of our presence, and inquired where we were going. I informed them that we were rebel soldiers, belonging to the infantry, but we were going up into the valley to join General Rhoddy, for he was a fighting man. After finishing our supper we offered him pay for it, but he would not receive a cent, and expressed himself glad to think that we were going to join

Rhoddy. I then inquired if he knew where we would find the pickets stationed, and he informed me that the first picket was stationed on this side of the creek, not more than four hundred yards from his house, and that two of them had taken tea with him that evening.

I then asked him if the pickets had instructions to fire on any one approaching after dark without first halting them. He replied that they had not, and that when halted to halloo out "all right," and advance boldly. We then started down the hill, toward the creek, laughing and talking, with the understanding that when the proper time arrived, and I should give a certain signal, to draw our revolvers and demand their surrender. Upon reaching the foot of the hill we were halted and challenged. After answering in the usual manner, and adding that it was "all right," we were told to advance, which we did, and when sufficiently near I discovered there were but two of them. They inquired who we were, and I told them the same tale I had told the doctor, and gave them to understand that I knew they were here—that I had been informed so by the doctor, up at the house; in fact I made myself very familiar with them, and taking a seat upon a rock seemed to feel quite at home. They inquired if we had any arms, and we told them we had not. If they had searched us they would have found two navy revolvers concealed about the person of us both.

After obtaining all the information required about the disposition of Rhoddy's forces, and their contemplated movements, we also learned that their reserve picket was on the opposite side of the creek, which they crossed in a small boat, and that they would be relieved in about an hour, when they would ferry us over. After remaining as long as I thought it prudent I gave the signal, when we each drew a revolver and demanded their surrender, and, on peril of their lives, not to speak above a whisper.

After securing their arms we marched them before us up the hill, and halted at the doctor's house. All this proceeding had taken considerable time, and the men I had left behind becoming alarmed at our lengthy stay had come up to the house, arousing the inmates a second time, and inquired if any Confederate soldiers had been there that evening. The old doctor told them that he had not seen one for more than a week. On reaching the house with the prisoners I found my men there. The old doctor looked at me and my party with the utmost astonishment. I now informed the old gentleman that we would have to draw on him for two horses for the prisoners to ride, knowing that we would be pursued before morning.

At this request he produced his oath of allegiance and protection papers, signed by General Rosecrans. I told him to come down to Corinth and we would settle it. Without any further interruption or delay we proceeded to the latter place, and reported to headquarters. A few days after this the old doctor sent one of his neighbours in to see General Dodge, and have his horses returned to him. I had stated to the general all I knew respecting the doctor's loyalty, and the general sent the agent back as he came, without them. Not long after this latter trip one of my outside scouts sent me word that Captain Shackleford, of the Twenty-Sixth Mississippi Infantry, who lived twenty-eight miles south of Corinth, had returned home on leave of absence. I immediately started out, taking with me five of my men, arriving next morning, and surrounding his house before daylight. We found the captain and two soldiers, all of whom surrendered to us without any resistance. After securing their horses, arms, &c., we mounted them, and brought them all safe into camp.

During all this time my scouts and couriers were operating in their different departments, with entire success, in obtaining the Southern papers, and also valuable information. Occasionally I would lose a man, either by capture or by being killed. Their services were invaluable to the generals, and were appreciated; they expressed themselves fully satisfied.

About the first of October General Dodge requested me to ascertain at what point the Tennessee River could be forded above Eastport. This was the first intimation that I had of the intended movement of our army towards Chattanooga, Middle Tennessee. Three days after I reported to the general that the river could be forded at Green's Bluff, one mile above the mouth of Town Creek, and one mile below the mouth of the Big Nancy, on the opposite side.

I now found it necessary to make some disposition of my wife. My friend Bennett was about to start for Illinois with his family, and I concluded to send my wife under his care.

The grand move of our army had now commenced. General Sherman and his command were already on the march. General Dodge was ordered to follow, my scouts, under my charge, constituting the advance guard for his command, taking the road leading to Pulaski, Tennessee. General Sherman had moved by the way of Florence.

I had received orders to scout the country in every direction, and secure all serviceable horses and mules. We had been out several days when I learned that a number of Confederate scouts were in our advance. I started out with my men, determined to overtake and capture them, if possible. Four of my men and myself were dressed in the Confederate uniform, and occupied the advance. On reaching a crossroad we came upon them. At a considerable distance off they saw us, and demanded to know to what command we belonged. I answered, "Confederate." This announcement did not seem to satisfy them, for without any hesitation they pulled away at us.

My company had received orders to keep within supporting distance of us, which they were at that time. I at once ordered them to charge, which they did, the enemy scattering in all directions, and my men also separating and pursuing them in the same manner. I soon found myself alone, and in hot pursuit of a single rebel. I was well mounted, and after a chase of about a mile my man dismounted and ran into a house. I followed him closely; at the same time I saw three or four of my men coming up the road at full speed.

As I ran up to the door I was met by a nice looking young lady, who asked me if the Yankees were after me. I told her they were, and asked her if she could tell me where to hide. She told me she did not know. I then inquired where the other man was, and she replied that he was up stairs. She then opened a door leading to a room, and I ran into it, she following. Just then my men arrived, and were at the door demanding where in h—l them d——d rebels had gone that came in the house. The young lady had told me to stoop down in the corner, and standing before me screened me from their view by spreading out her crinoline. She told them they had gone out the back door, and as she finished speaking away they went, pell-mell through the hall, out at the back door, and had soon disappeared in the rear of the house. I now relieved the young lady, and could scarcely contain myself, I was so full of laughter. In a few minutes my men returned, when I told them that the man was upstairs, whom they soon found.

Nothing more occurred after this, except skirmishing and the capture of a few prisoners each day, until we arrived at Pulaski, where General Dodge received orders to repair the Nashville and Huntsville railroad, establishing his headquarters at Pulaski. General Sherman had by this time taken Lookout Mountain.

It was now about the tenth of November. Our forces were scattered along the line of railroad from Columbia to Huntsville, Ala. At this time there were but a very few rebels in that vicinity. My time was principally employed with my men, scouring the country in quest of horses, mules, etc., occasionally an incident occurring of a startling and amusing nature. I had learned that the rebel General Rhoddy was with his command in the Tuscumbia valley, with his headquarters established at Tuscumbia. He also had possession of some points along the river in the vicinity of Florence. Captain Phillips, with the Ninth Illinois mounted infantry, had almost daily skirmishing with them along the river. I had sent out some of my scouts in various directions; one of them returned, stating that two wagon loads of salt were at Lamb's Ferry.

I took five of my men and started with the intention of destroying it, which we did near the river, within forty miles of Pulaski. On our return, and during the night time (which was very cool), we stopped, putting up at a wealthy planter's, who professed to be a good Union man. After stabling and feeding our horses and partaking of a good supper we retired to rest, feeling perfectly secure, being only twenty-seven miles from our army. At the same time, I took the necessary precaution to keep one man on picket. About twelve o'clock (midnight) we were aroused by our guard, who told us the yard was full of rebel cavalry. I ordered the boys to get up, and without making any noise to dress and prepare their guns for instant use. I could then hear considerable noise in the parlour, which was the adjoining room. After all was ready, I ordered two of the men to step out on the porch and slip around to the back window, and, if necessary, to fire in through it, but not until they saw me enter from the inside through the door. Taking the other four men, each one with his revolver in hand, I approached the door and gently opening it I discovered six rebel officers seated around a fire.

I at once demanded a surrender, to which they complied without any resistance, but very much astonished at our unexpected appearance. They ranked from a second lieutenant up to a major, which somewhat surprised me in turn. I afterwards learned they were a portion of Morgan's command, who were trying to make their escape, which was just after his defeat. We secured their arms and horses, keeping close guard over them until morning, when we started for camp, where we arrived safely with our prisoners and captured property, which pleased General Dodge very much.

A few days after the above occurrence, I sent out two of my scouts, dressed in Confederate uniform. While on their return to camp they met a young man dressed in rebel uniform, whom they conscripted for the rebel army. The young man was very indignant at first, and told them they were doing wrong, that he was on special business from

General Bragg, all of which was of no avail, my scouts persisted in taking him before their Captain, who could act at his pleasure. They then demanded his arms which he hesitated for some time before delivering up, and said he did not believe they were Confederate soldiers, he would never give them up, that the whole Federal army could not take them from him alive.

They had now approached to within about two miles of our camp, when this young man discovered that he was a prisoner in the hand of Federal scouts. He attempted to escape by putting spurs to his horse, but the scouts were on the watch, and the moment he made the effort one of the men caught his horse by the bridle rein. He was taken to headquarters, and upon examining his person was found a water-proof haversack filled with letters and papers for General Bragg. Among them was a despatch from General Bragg's chief of scouts in Middle Tennessee, giving the exact number of men in General Dodge's command, together with all his late orders and a late paper from Nashville. Other papers were found proving this young man to be a spy. The general then turned him over to me, with orders to deliver him to the provost marshal and to have him put into a cell, also, to tell him, that he had only a few days to live; except on one condition would his life be spared, that was, to tell who the person was that furnished him with those papers. He replied, that he would not confess anything. That when he entered the army he did not expect to live through this war, and if Tennessee could not be restored to the Southern Confederacy he would rather die than live. I could not but admire his brave manly spirit.

At no time, while in my presence, did he seem to feel depressed. The next day a commission was called to give him a trial. The prisoner was called out, who confessed to the charge preferred against him. He was sentenced to be hung on the following Friday. When he was taken to the scaffold I was permitted to talk to him. I addressed him thus; "Davis, you are not the man that should be hung, and if you would yet tell me who General Bragg's chief of scouts was, so I might capture him, your life would yet be spared." He looked me steadily in the eye, and said—"do you suppose were I your friend that I would betray you?" I told him I did not know, but life was sweet to all men. His reply to this, was, "Sir, if you think I am that kind of a man you have missed your mark. You may hang me a thousand times and I would not betray my friends."

I then left him, only to witness in less than two minutes afterwards his fall from the scaffold, a dead man. Thus ended the life of Samuel Davis, one of General Bragg's scouts, a noble, brave young man, who possessed principle. I have often regretted the fate of this young man, who could brave such a death when his life rested in his own hands. His mind was one of principle, though engaged in a wrong cause.

Guerrillas were becoming more numerous, and receiving information from two of my scouts that a force of rebels, moving north, had crossed the river at Lamb's ferry; I reported the same to the general, and he ordered me to take my scouts and see if it was so. I started with eleven men, and, after proceeding about twelve miles, in the direction spoken of, we saw six mounted rebels emerge into the road in our front, and form a line across the road. We immediately ordered a charge, when they fired a volley, turned about and retreated in hot haste. We were mounted on good fleet horses, and very soon began to overtake them, picking them up, one at a time.

After chasing them about half a mile, my men succeeded in picking up all but two of them. I still continued the chase followed by six of my men, the remainder having halted some distance in the rear with the prisoners. On reaching the top of a hill, under full headway, I unexpectedly found the road full of rebels, forming in line of battle, and not more than twenty yards in our front. There was but one course to pursue, and that was to charge through. In fact, it was impossible so check our horses, and away we went, firing our revolvers right and left. The rebels were thrown into confusion by this unexpected appearance in their midst, and thought the whole Federal army was charging them. It was now each man for himself, and through them we went. The next question was to get away from them, and the only chance was to wheel about and return as we came. No sooner said than away we went, charging about three hundred and fifty men, formerly Rhoddy's old regiment, commanded, at this time, by Lieut.-Col. Johnson.

A portion of them had formed a line and, as we passed them, they fired a volley into us, wounding three. One rebel stood beside the road and, as I came up, levelled his revolver within two inches of my head and fired, the ball just grazing my neck, and powder burning my face and singing my hair. We had now returned back, still keeping under full headway, while the rebels continued to fire after us, but not daring to pursue. We soon came up with the rest of my men, who had remained with the prisoners, and, without any delay, we retraced our way to camp, all arriving safely, and feeling rejoiced that we had escaped so well. My wound was not of a serious nature. My two companions, however, were less fortunate, one having his arm broken, and the other his thigh fractured.

As soon as we arrived in camp I reported to the general, who ordered out a detachment of the Seventh and Ninth Illinois Mounted Infantry, who were to find and attack this rebel force, if possible, but they returned without finding them, for the rebels had retreated and re-crossed the Tennessee River.

My wound now began to trouble me, and I applied to the General for leave of absence, to visit my family up North. I now felt that I had had my fill of satisfaction. The following is a correct copy of the Special Order relieving me from duty for a certain time:

Headquarters Left-Wing Sixteenth Army Corps,
Pulaski, Tennessee, Dec. 15th, 1863.

Special Order,
No. 39.

VI. L. H. N——, in employ of United States Government, is hereby ordered to Illinois, on business for this command. The Q. M. Department will furnish transportation. He will turn over his quartermaster and ordinance stores to James Hansel, taking proper receipts therefore. During N——'s absence James Hansel will act as Chief of Scouts.

By order of
Brig.-Gen. G. M. Dodge.
J. W. Barner,
Lieut. and A. A. A. G.

After making preparations, I started for Nashville, remaining there about one week. My health was not good and I experienced considerable pain in my wound. I had been in Nashville but a few days when I found one of my old scouts, who had been absent from me a long time. While stationed at Pulaski, during the month of November, I sent out three of my best scouts, with instructions to reconnoitre up and down the Tennessee River. After being absent about three weeks, one of them, Biffell, a Tennessean by birth, returned. He was wounded through the shoulder, and reported as follows: After scouting along the river four or five days, finding that they were going to be arrested or pursued, they began to retrace their steps. Being very weary they stopped at a plantation, about midnight, to feed and rest.

They were at some distance from the house, at the lower end of the plantation. After feeding their horses, they crept into a corn-crib, and, laying down, were soon asleep. The first intimation they had of danger they were aroused and found themselves surrounded by nine men, who had their guns levelled upon them. They surrendered, without any resistance, and were marched back to the Tennessee River, where it was decided they should be hung. They declared that they were Rhoddy's scouts, when it was decided to send them to Rhoddy.

After crossing the Tennessee River, their guards were reduced to five men. They halted at a plantation to feed and rest. The prisoners now fully determined to escape—knowing that if they were carried before General Rhoddy they would be recognized by some of his men, and certain death would await them. One of the party had kept concealed, in his boot, a small revolver. While three of the guard were in the house, eating dinner, the other two remained on guard. Two of the prisoners then seized the guns belonging to the guard while the other drew his revolver from his boot leg, but it would not fire—the caps being damp. He then struck one of the guards over the head with his pistol, knocking him down, while the other was knocked down with a musket.

By this time the three men in the house were alarmed, by the noise, and made their appearance, only to see their two bleeding comrades lying on the ground, and the prisoners making the best possible use of their legs in crossing a corn field. The three guards commenced firing on them, and wounded Biffles, who then became separated from his companions—whom he saw no more.

This ended Biffle's narrative, and, until my arrival at Nashville, I had not heard anything of the other two—Joe, from Mississippi, and Haines, of the Second Iowa Infantry. One morning, while in the quartermaster's depot, at Nashville, I was asked by a gentleman to what command I belonged. I told him, General Dodge's scouts, and he then said that one of the d——d'st looking cases he had ever seen was then up at the Soldier's Home; that he had arrived that morning, from the vicinity of Chattanooga, and professed to belong to General Dodge's scouts. It occurred to me at once, after hearing the description of this strange looking being, that it must be either Joe or Haines. Without any delay, I proceeded to the Soldiers' Home, and about the first man I saw was Haines, and, true enough, he was a hard looking case, reduced almost to a skeleton, covered with dirt and rags.

Pen cannot describe the meeting that there took place. He was overjoyed at seeing me, and clasped his arms around me and caressed me like a child. I immediately took him to the barbershop and had him shaved and shampooed. I also procured an order for a suit of clothes, after which I presented him to Generals Sherman and Dodge, who were then in the city, stopping at the St. Cloud Hotel. They received him kindly and heard his report. He furnished me the following narrative. I will commence at the time they had knocked the guard down and effected their escape, by running across the cornfield—when they became separated from Biffles.

After making their escape, they concluded to make their way toward Corinth—Joe being familiar with the country—though they were, at this time, in the midst of Rhoddy's scattered forces. Rhoddy, having learned the circumstances, had sent out detachments of men, in various directions, to watch for them, and, after travelling two days and nights, without provisions, they were discovered by his cavalry. After running some distance, they came to a narrow defile. Haines, having now become so exhausted that he could proceed no further, told Joe to go ahead and try to make his escape, and that he would get behind a stump—having yet in his possession one of the guns taken from the guard, but no percussion caps.

Joe continued running, while Haines, took up a position behind a stump and, as the pursuers came up within fifty yards he levelled his gun at them, and they retreated. Thus it continued until they succeeded in flanking him, when he arose to a standing position and, breaking his gun over a stump, surrendered. Joe, in the meantime, had effected his escape from this party, and has not been heard of by me up to this time.

Haines, now a prisoner, was conveyed to Tuscumbia, where he was recognized as one of the men who killed the guard, and was ordered to be put in heavy irons. After keeping him closely confined for several days, orders were received to remove all the prisoners to Rome, Georgia. As the Federals were advancing into the valley at that time, Haines was taken along handcuffed. As they were taking their departure, the provost marshal told the captain of the guard that he would hold him strictly responsible for that man, as he was a desperado, and if he made his escape he would have to take his place.

After marching several days across the sand mountains, they came to the Coosa River, near Rome, at which time he said he was nearly in a state of starvation. While seated on the river bank, waiting for the boat which was to convey them to Cahawba, a young lady made her appearance, carrying a basket of eatables, consisting of pies and cakes, and, addressing him kindly, asked him to eat some of her pies. He told her that he had no money, but she replied that he must eat some anyhow, saying that she did not want any pay from him. (She had been informed that he was a Federal spy, and was to be shot.) He then asked her name and where she lived. She told him her name and said that she lived with her brother-in-law, some distance out west, also telling his name. After eating abundantly of her pies and cakes, he felt very much refreshed. This young lady appeared to him like an angel sent to soothe and relieve his troubled mind. She was the first person who had shown any sympathy toward him since his capture.

The boat now making its appearance he was ordered aboard, and was chained, by the captain of the guard, to one of the uprights of the boat. A lieutenant who was on the boat, at the time of her landing at this point, on passing Haines saw that he was chained, and, without consulting any person, released him, saying that it was a shame and not right to chain a man on water. Immediately after this, the captain of the guard, in passing, saw that Haines was released, and immediately rechained him, cursing and swearing at the lieutenant, and threatening to report him.

After dark, the lieutenant, watching for an opportunity, told Haines that, if he would jump overboard, he would relieve him of his chains and break his handcuffs—that he would let the d— n captain see if he could treat a man in that manner. Haines, of course, consented, and the lieutenant managed to release him, without being observed, which was no sooner done than Haines made one jump, and plunged headlong into the Coosa River, on the west side of the boat, and swam ashore, nearly chilled to death by the cold.

After scrambling up the bank, he proceeded north, finding himself in a wild, barren and mountainous country. After travelling all that night and the next day, until late in the evening, without any food, except roots and wild herbs, he unexpectedly, upon gaining the top of a high ridge, and looking down into the valley below, saw with inexpressible joy, the smoke curling up through the tree tops, and upon closer observation, he could see a few log houses and people moving about. Being hungry and nearly naked, he resolved to venture, at all hazards, so moving cautiously, he approached the house from the rear, and had got within one hundred yards when he perceived a female emerge from it and approach the spot where he lay concealed. Upon seeing her face what was his inexpressible joy and astonishment at beholding the kind-hearted lady who had furnished him with pies and cakes, on the banks of the Coosa River.

He at once attracted her attention, and she, in turn, was surprised at seeing him there. She told him that she would bring him some food and clothing, but that as the country was full of rebel cavalry, he must lay concealed through the day. After dark she went to him, accompanied by her brother-in-law, who told him to keep secluded all the next day, and the next night he would convey him fifteen miles and turn him over to other friends. This promise he faithfully kept, and the second party conveyed him to within a few miles of the Tennessee River, and gave him instructions necessary to enable him to avoid danger, and the course to pursue to reach Nashville. The reader is already acquainted with his arrival and condition.

Shortly after meeting my old friend Haines, I took my departure for the North, arriving in Illinois the first day of January, 1864, where I found my wife and family all well, and happy at seeing me alive once more. I remained at home until the first day of October, when I started for Tennessee. In the meantime, I had learned that General Dodge had been wounded and was absent from his command, which was the reason for my visiting Memphis. It had also been reported to me that he was coming to the latter place, to assume command of that department, and I was anxious to again tender him my services. In this I was disappointed. I found General Washburne in command, and also learned that General Dodge was assigned to the command of Missouri, with headquarters at St. Louis.

I at once tendered my services to General Washburne, and they were accepted, for a short time. The General, however, told me that he would not remain long in Memphis, and recommended me to the notice of Brig.-Gen. Grierson, to whom I at once reported. I was greatly surprised at meeting my old friend, S. L. Woodward, formerly General Sherman's Chief Clerk, now Captain and Acting Adjutant General on General Grierson's staff, who was pleased to see me. My services were at once accepted by the General, who was making preparations to send a cavalry force into Mississippi, to tap the Mobile and Ohio railroad south of Corinth.

This expedition was entrusted to the command of General Grierson, who questioned me respecting the roads, streams, &c. I told the general that I could guide him and his command through the proposed route without having to swim a horse over any steam of water. On the morning of the twenty-first of December, 1864, the expedition left Memphis, Tennessee. It was comprised of three brigades. The first was commanded by Colonel Karge, and was composed of the Second New Jersey, Fourth Missouri, Seventh Indiana and First Mississippi Mounted Rifles. The second brigade, commanded by Colonel Winslow, included the Third and Fourth Iowa and Tenth Missouri.

The third brigade, commanded by Colonel Osborne, consisted of the Fourth and Eleventh Illinois, Second Wisconsin, Third U. S. Coloured and fifty men of the Pioneer Corps, coloured, commanded by Lieutenant Lewis, of the Seventh Indiana Cavalry, numbering in all about thirty-three hundred men. The whole commanded by Brig.-Gen. B. H. Grierson. His staff consisted of the following members: Major M. H. Williams, Tenth Missouri Cavalry, Acting Assistant Inspector General, and Captain S. L. Woodward, Assistant Adjutant General, U. S. A., accompanied by a telegraph operator, whose quick hand is lightning.

Previous to the departure of this expedition, reliable information had been received, from scouts, that the enemy were accumulating a large quantity of supplies on the line of the Mobile and Ohio railroad and Mississippi Central railroad, for transportation to Hood's army. On the morning of the nineteenth, a brigade was sent forward, to make a demonstration toward Bolivar, and thence to swing south-east and join the main column near Ripley, Mississippi, but owing to heavy rains on that and several previous days, it was impossible to cross Wolf River, and, therefore, the intended junction could not be effected, and the command returned to Memphis.

On the morning of the twenty-first, the expedition started from Memphis, accompanied by a considerable force of infantry, moving along the line of the Memphis and Charleston railroad, as far as Moscow, making a demonstration toward Corinth. The cavalry, under General Grierson, cut loose from the infantry near Germantown, and pursued the most direct route for Ripley, passing through Lamar and Salem.

From Early Grove, a detachment of one hundred men, commanded by Captain Neet, of the Tenth Missouri, was ordered to proceed to the neighbourhood of Grand Junction, and cut the railroad and telegraph lines there. He regained the command between Salem and Ripley, having successfully accomplished the work assigned him.

The transportation for the expedition consisted of pack mules, carrying ten days' rations, and one hundred rounds per man of extra ammunition. No artillery, ambulances or wagons accompanied the expedition. Such encumbrances, which have proved fatal to so many well contemplated raids, were dispensed with, that the command might be able to move with great rapidity. General Grierson's orders from General Dana were to cut the Mobile and Ohio railroad effectually, if possible. Further than this the general was at liberty to use his own discretion—and the sequel will show with what masterly skill it was exercised. The march to Ripley was unopposed, very few of the enemy being seen.

Arriving at the latter place in time for dinner, on the twenty-fourth, two detachments of the Second New Jersey, under the command of Major Van Rensalaer, were immediately sent out with orders to proceed to Booneville, on the Mobile and Ohio Railroad, to destroy it and the government property there, and rejoin the command at Ellistown, twenty miles south of Ripley. I was ordered to accompany this expedition as guide. The other detachment of two hundred men, under the command of Captain Search, of the Fourth Illinois, was to strike the same road at Gunntown, and rejoin the command at Ellistown.

This the detachments successfully accomplished, the former capturing and destroying a large quantity of quartermaster stores, five cars, cutting the telegraph, burning railroad bridges and trestle-work, and paroling about twenty prisoners. At the same time the attention of the enemy at Corinth was diverted from the proceedings. They were led to anticipate an attack on that place. The track and the telegraph line were destroyed at Gunntown. While this was being done the main column, after a few hours' rest, left Ripley and moved rapidly toward Tupelo, arriving there on the afternoon of the twenty-fifth without meeting with any opposition.

From this place the Eleventh Illinois, Lieut.-Col. Funk, commanding, was sent to destroy a bridge and some trestle-work over the Old Town Creek. In the meantime Colonel Karge was ordered to move rapidly upon Verona Station, seven miles south, with his entire brigade, information having been obtained that a force of seven hundred dismounted cavalry, belonging to Forrest's command, were stationed at that place, guarding an immense amount of quartermaster stores. About ten o'clock that evening a gallant charge was made into the place, led by the Seventh Indiana Cavalry, Captain Skelton, commanding.

The surprise was so complete that little resistance was offered, most of the garrison, aided by the darkness, escaping into the timber.

This affair resulted in the easy capture of eight buildings filled with fixed ammunition, variously estimated at from 250 to 300 tons, 5000 stand of new carbines, 8000 sacks of shelled corn, a large quantity of wheat, an immense amount of quartermaster stores, clothing, camp and garrison equipage, a train of sixteen cars, and two hundred army wagons, the same that were captured by Forrest from General Sturgis, at his disastrous defeat near Gunntown the June previous.

After effectually destroying all this property, tearing up the track, burning the bridges and cutting the telegraph wire, the brigade started to rejoin the command, leaving a fire in their rear for miles. The explosion of ammunition, which continued at intervals all night, added much to this magnificent scene, which must have produced a peculiar effect upon the minds of the citizens, who were not aware of our presence.

On the morning of the twenty-sixth the command moved out from Tupelo. The third brigade was ordered to proceed down the railroad and destroy the bridges, trestle-work, water-tanks, etc. On arriving at Shannon they surprised and captured a large train of cars, containing one hundred new army wagons on the way for Forrest's forces, besides a quantity of quartermaster and commissary stores, and also several government buildings, all of which were destroyed. After the main column arrived at this place the third brigade was relieved by the second, which received orders to proceed down the railroad, destroying it as they went. The remainder of the command kept the public road leading toward Okolona, and camped that night on Chawappa Creek.

On the morning of the twenty-seventh the command moved out at an early hour, the second brigade in advance. After proceeding a few miles the enemy was encountered. They numbered about one hundred men, who kept falling back and exchanging shots with our advance guard, just as we came in sight of Okolona. Here a rebel courier was captured, bearing a dispatch for the captain commanding the post. The dispatch stated that thirteen hundred infantry would reinforce him, arriving by railroad from Mobile.

While making preparations for the fight I sent one of my comrades into Okolona, who returned with a favorable report. The same scout was sent from this place with a dispatch to Memphis, for General Dana. He succeeded in arriving safely with it, but had some narrow escapes. He was arrested once, carried back and closely searched, but no papers were found and he was permitted to proceed, telling them that he was a good rebel. Being acquainted with many of the citizens of that county his story was believed. He was nick-named "Perseverance."

A fight was now anticipated, and the order was given to form squadrons. The command "forward" was sounded. It was a grand sight to witness the cavalry moving along in perfect order over the prairie, with banners gaily fluttering in the breeze, each company bearing its guidon. Peaceable possession was taken of the town, a large quantity of commissary stores and several thousand pounds of finished leather captured and destroyed, and sufficient tobacco obtained to supply the whole command. The telegraph wire was tapped at this point, and dispatches were intercepted from General Dick Taylor, Maj.-Gen. Gardiner and others, ordering the commanding officer at Egypt to hold that place at all hazards, and intimating that reinforcements would be sent from Mobile and other points. The promised reinforcements soon made their appearance. A long train of cars was seen approaching from the south. When within two miles of town they could see the burning buildings, and they concluded to retreat to Egypt Station, ten miles south. After effectually destroying all the government property the command moved to within five miles of Egypt and camped for the night.

During the night several deserters came into our lines, bringing with them their guns. They said they belonged to our army, had been prisoners a long time, and had joined the Confederate army in order to avoid a lingering and horrible death in the prison pen at Andersonville, Ga. As soon as this fact became known among the men they at once conferred upon them the title of "Galvanized Confeds." These men stated that the rebels offered inducements to all those of foreign birth who would join them, promising that they should be required to do only garrison duty. They further stated that about two hundred of their own stamp were in the stockade at Egypt, and would be compelled to fight us in the morning if attacked. The morning came, and at an early hour the command started for Egypt. The general did not anticipate a fight there, but was under the impression that the rebels would evacuate.

However, the opposite fact was soon ascertained, and the whole command, except the Fourth Iowa, was ordered to move by the wagon-road; the latter regiment moved down the railroad. The second brigade was ordered to follow as a reserve. They had not proceeded far before a squad of mounted rebels was seen; they kept retreating, and occasionally exchanged a shot with our advance. The command soon emerged from the timber into the open prairie, where were plainly visible to the eye, about a mile distant, the few houses, depot, and stockade, which comprise the town or station of Egypt. On nearer approach it was discovered by the third brigade that Colonel Karge, commanding first brigade, had come well up to the enemy's works, and heavy skirmishing was going on. General Grierson and staff accompanied the first brigade.

A train of cars stood on the track, and a four-gun battery was mounted on one of them; all were within supporting distance of the garrison. The enemy's skirmishers were driven into their works, where they were well protected, while our forces were exposed on the open prairie. While forming the troops for a charge a movement was discovered which led the General to suppose that the train was about to leave. He at once ordered Colonel Karge to charge the works. Drawing his sabre he ordered a detachment of the Fourth Missouri and Seventh Indiana to follow him, and away he dashed for the train, which was by this time moving off. So closely did the general, his staff and escort press them, that the engineer detached fourteen cars, leaving them in our possession—thus escaping with the battery, which was attached next the tender.

An exciting chase was now kept up for nearly a mile, the cavalry firing rapidly their carbines and revolvers, while the gunners threw grape, canister and shell. It was soon discovered that two other trains were approaching from the south. They were loaded with troops. Captain Woodward, General Grierson's assistant adjutant-general, a young, brave and dashing cavalry officer, was ordered to take the detachment that had been chasing the train and proceed down the road rapidly and tear up the track. This he successfully accomplished, preventing the trains from approaching nearer than within two miles of the station, and keeping in check General Gardiner, with reinforcements to the number of about two thousand infantry.

The captain was ably assisted by Captain Hencke, of the Fourth Missouri, and Captains Elliott and Skelton, of the Seventh Indiana. The former fell wounded while charging the enemy, who had disembarked, thrown out a line of skirmishers, and begun to advance. The captain, with only one hundred men, fell back from the railroad, the infantry pursuing. When about six hundred yards from the train Captain Woodward ordered a left about, and with a will and a spirit stirring yell he charged them, driving them back in confusion. His loss was two men killed and five or six wounded, and thirty horses killed.

While this brave little band was so gallantly fighting the first brigade charged the enemy. The charge was made by the Second New Jersey, Lieut.-Col. Yorke, their brave commander, leading the attack. Mounted on their horses they charged right up to the stockade, so that they could fire directly into the garrison. They were armed with that splendid carbine, the Spencer seven shooter, and poured, in quick succession, volley after volley into their ranks. The rebels could not withstand the fire. They were flanked on both sides, while the third brigade lay back in the rear not more than sixty yards, dismounted and ready to participate in making a charge. The charge was not necessary; the rebels saw that there was no chance for retreat, and that their reinforcements could not reach them; they therefore surrendered the whole garrison to Lieut.-Col. Yorke.

The prisoners numbered about eight hundred, infantry and cavalry. Their loss in killed and wounded was not less than sixty or seventy. Among the killed were Brig.-Gen. Gohlston, commanding post, and a colonel. Our loss was fifteen killed and seventy wounded, thirty of whom had to be left behind. Over one hundred horses were killed at Egypt, and one thousand stand of arms captured and burned with the cars. After burying the dead and caring for the wounded the command moved west and southwest toward Houston. The prisoners were taken along.

This fight was a very spirited one, and reflects great credit upon the officers and men engaged. It has been seldom, if ever before during this rebellion, that a charge has been made and successfully carried out by a mounted force against an equal force protected by a stockade. General Grierson participated in the victory with his brave followers, and complimented them very highly. Just as the garrison surrendered the rebel General Gardiner and his force left on their trains, retreating towards West Point. Beside the fourteen cars mentioned that were abandoned, ten more were captured at the station. They were loaded with two large pontoon bridges, shelled corn and quartermaster stores, all on the way for Hood's army.

I do not think it had been the intention of General Grierson to attack this place, and I believe he did so principally with a view to the recapture of our own men, who appeared to feel very much rejoiced at their deliverance. He hinted that the capture of so many prisoners had saved the command several days hard riding, as he would now be compelled to take them to Vicksburg. The general governs his actions according to circumstances, being quick both to plan and to act. On the night of the 28th the command camped within three miles of Houston, on the plantation of Norton & Co. They remarked that we were the first Yankees they had ever seen, and that "weuns" looked like their folks. General Grierson somewhat surprised the ladies by displaying his musical talent on the piano, after which one of the ladies favoured the General and staff with one of Longfellow's beautiful songs, "Hiawatha."

At its conclusion one of the officers complimented her by saying that he thought the song very beautiful, and that her singing was excellent. She replied that she did not suppose he would like it, as it was seldom appreciated except by persons of literary tastes. This was said as a compliment to the Captain, she being under the impression that the Northerners were an ignorant race, and was surprised to meet any one possessing a cultivated taste in the Yankee army.

The next morning the General missed his saddle blanket, when, in the way of a joke, I suppose, he remarked to the inmates that he thought it was not treating him well to steal his blanket, when he had taken so much pains to guard their property. So I thought, also, especially in view of the fact that there was not a chicken or turkey left alive on the plantation.

On the morning of the twenty-ninth, the whole command moved out, passing through Houston, from which place two detachments were sent—one south-east, toward West Point, and the other north, toward Pontotac—for the purpose of misleading the enemy. On returning, they destroyed the bridge across the Houlka River. Orders were soon issued to the command to sequestrate, for the use of the prisoners—who were in a pitiable condition—all the blankets, shoes and such clothing as was required, that might be met with. Nothing worthy of note transpired this day, and the command camped at Hohenlinden.

Morning of the thirtieth, left camp at an early hour and proceeded to Bellefontaine, capturing a few prisoners, among whom was the notorious Captain Tom Ford, whose business it had been, for the past two years, to conscript and hunt down—with bloodhounds—good Union men, and who confessed to having assisted in hanging several of them. He was placed in custody of a special guard, but, by some means, succeeded in making his escape. From Bellefontaine a detachment was sent toward Starkville, again threatening the Mobile and Ohio railroad, while one hundred and fifty men, under Captain Beckwith, of the Fourth Iowa, were sent to Bankston, where they arrived at midnight.

They found the place quiet—the inhabitants having had no intimation of the Yankees being in their vicinity. At this place a large manufacturing establishment, which was turning out one thousand yards of cloth and two thousand pair of shoes per day, was completely burned down. It was working five hundred hands. A large supply of cloth, shoes, cotton, wool and commissary and quartermaster's stores were also destroyed. A large flouring mill underwent the same fate. The following incident will show how completely the enemy was surprised.

Just as the fire got well started, the superintendent of the factory made his appearance, in his night clothes, swearing, threatening to arrest the guard and night watchers, and wanting to know what in h—l they were about that they did not extinguish the fire. It was amusing to hear him, and still more so to witness his astonishment when he discovered who and what we were. The captain perceiving his mistake, told him that the night was so very cold, that he had concluded to have a fire. "H—l and d—nation," said the man, "would you burn up the manufactory to make a fire to warm by?"

On the morning of the thirty-first, left camp at six o'clock, the first brigade in advance. At about nine o'clock, the command was joined by Captain Beckwith, who returned from Bankston, reporting his complete success. The column proceeded along the Bellefontaine and Middletown road, passing through a hilly country, and arriving at Lodi about eleven o'clock in the morning. At that place we captured seven hundred and ninety fat hogs, which were *en route* for Hood's army, and also two thousand bushels of wheat, which was at once destroyed. After a good deal of speculation, and about one thousand and one ideas being advanced, as to what disposition should be made of the grunting stock, it was finally concluded to drive it before us. This was done amid a good deal of fun. Just imagine about eight hundred hogs before you, in the road, and about two hundred jolly fellows driving them, and then picture to yourself the various remarks and expressions they used. The general and staff participated in the fun, and directed the movements.

After putting the hogs through for five miles, they being found to be too troublesome, it was decided, by a council of officers, to put them all to death. They were too fat to be driven further, averaging, as they did, two hundred and fifty pounds each. The men constructed a large pen, and into it they were driven. The idea was then advanced after killing to burn them. This being decided about a whole brigade dismounted and, with drawn sabres, charged in among the squealing herd, splitting each of them open in the back. They then piled rails upon them, which were fired. This soon made a glorious barbecue. H. V., a clerk declared that, a few years hence, new discoveries would be made in that section of the country, in the shape of lard oil wells—the genuine oil. According to Mobile prices, pork was worth, at that time, five dollars a pound.

While the destruction of hogs was going on, Colonel Karge commanding the first brigade, was moving toward Middletown. He struck the Mississippi Central railroad within one mile north of Winona, cutting the railroad and telegraph. Before cutting the wires Colonel Karge intercepted a dispatch, which contained an inquiry respecting the operation of Wirt Adams, at Canton—whether he had sent any reinforcements up the road? A reply could not be obtained. Nine locomotives were destroyed at Winona, and also the depot and a large quantity of quartermaster stores. From this place the command proceeded to Middletown and camped for the night, with the exception of the Third Iowa, commanded by Colonel Noble. After feeding, and resting a few hours, this regiment was ordered to proceed up the road to Grenada, and to destroy the bridges on the route and all government property in that place, after doing which he was to rejoin the command at Benton, sixty-five miles south of Middletown. The distance from the latter place to Grenada is twenty-five miles.

On the morning of January 1st, 1865, the command left camp, the main column moving south, toward Benton, while the third brigade was sent down the Mississippi Central railroad, with orders to destroy it, and to rejoin the command at Benton. Nothing transpired on the march that day, worthy of notice, the main column camping that night within four miles of Lexington, Holmes County, Mississippi.

On the morning of the second we left camp, passing through Lexington. Some little skirmishing occurred in the advance, on the direct road to Ebenezer. We arrived there about noon, and passed through the town without halting. Shortly after leaving the place a rebel lieutenant belonging to the Fifth Texas Cavalry was captured. He stated that a force of rebel cavalry, numbering eleven thousand men, with artillery, was then at Benton, awaiting our approach. This story was not credited, at least it made no impression further than to increase our speed toward that point. About four o'clock, p.m., a dispatch was received from the second brigade, stating that they had moved down the railroad, which they destroyed as far as Gooman's, and then struck west through Franklin in the direction of Ebenezer. While at Franklin they were attacked by five or six hundred of Wirt Adam's cavalry, under the command of Colonel Woods.

After a very spirited fight the latter was repulsed with the loss of twenty-five killed and left on the field. Among them was one major and one captain, also several wounded; twenty prisoners were taken. Our loss was five killed and fourteen wounded. Too much praise cannot be awarded the whole brigade for their conduct in this fight, and particularly that of the Third U. S. Coloured Cavalry, commanded by Major Mann. They alone repulsed several desperate charges, having their adjutant killed and several wounded. Colonel Osband, commanding the brigade, is all fight. About six o'clock, p.m., the main column arrived at Benton, without meeting any opposition, and camped for the night. About ten o'clock, p.m., the third brigade arrived, having met with no opposition after their fight.

While the main force was lying at Benton Colonel Noble joined it. He came with tidings of success, that added largely to our victories. After destroying twenty-five miles of the Mississippi Central Railroad he surprised and took Grenada, where he captured four serviceable engines and ten others in process of repair, a very extensive machine shop, which had but recently been completed—the machinery for which was brought from Georgia—several buildings, containing immense quantities of commissary and quartermaster stores, twenty cases of Enfield rifles—which had been lately received for the purpose of arming the State militia—together with a considerable amount of ammunition.

Colonel Noble entered the office of the Grenada Picket, where he picked up a paper of the day previous, in which was an article stating that the Yankee raid on the Mobile and Ohio Railroad had played out, that Grierson's vandals had been repulsed and were making for Memphis with all speed. After reading this the colonel remarked to a citizen that it was not the intention of General Grierson to slight them so much as to fail in paying them a New Year's visit. He ordered the destruction of the Picket press, saying that if he could have done so consistently he would have left it untouched, so that the editors might proclaim what a warm call they had had from their Northern brethren.

The general now felt comparatively satisfied, as the main object of the expedition was to reach Benton without disaster. On the morning of the third the whole command left camp, proceeding southwest in the direction of Vicksburg, passing through Mechanicsburg. They arrived at the latter place before dark, camping there for the night. From this place, four scouts, members of the Fourth Iowa, were sent to Vicksburg, forty miles distant, with dispatches for General Washburne; also with a request that rations might be sent to Clear Creek.

On January fourth, we left camp at an early hour, and marched all day through canebrakes. Considerable bushwhacking was done this day, in which we lost one man killed—a member of the Third Iowa. The roads were good, but were not unlike the Mississippi River in one respect—they were very crooked, and were in a really God-forsaken country. We arrived at Clear Creek about five o'clock in the afternoon, having marched twenty-five miles. At this place we were met by the provision and forage train, which had been sent for the day previous.

Just as old Sol was disappearing behind the western horizon, our ears were greeted by the report of the sundown gun at Vicksburg, which had the effect of eliciting hearty cheers from our weary command. Captain Whiting, of General Washburne's staff, brought in the late Northern papers, containing news of the glorious successes of Sherman and Thomas. This night we camped within fifteen miles of Vicksburg, feeling perfectly secure and safe, after a sixteen day's ride through the enemy's country, and having travelled over five hundred miles. Our loss was twenty-five killed and eighty wounded—many of the latter slightly. We brought in six hundred prisoners, six hundred extra horses and mules, and about a thousand negroes. The amount of property destroyed cannot be estimated. It would take all the figures in the calendar, and the Philadelphia lawyers to sum it up. Seventy miles of railroad were effectually destroyed, with bridges, etc. Some private property was destroyed, not intentionally, but owing to its close proximity to burning rebel government property.

Too much praise cannot be awarded the four scouts who operated during this raid. Their services were duly appreciated by the generals. I have refrained somewhat from entering into details respecting myself, while on this raid, although I might make mention of many startling and amusing incidents that occurred. I occupied the advance all the time, of either detachments or the main column. At one time I had an exciting chase after three rebels, and fired three shots at them, but they, being mounted on fresh horses, succeeded in making their escape. I afterward learned that one of them was my own brother. I am only sorry that I did not succeed in taking him a prisoner. At one time I was within three miles of my home, and met with several of my old neighbours, many of whom expressed a strong desire that I should return and reside among them again—which I would willingly do could I be guaranteed a peaceable life, without changing my opinions respecting this rebellion.

The question of arming negroes was freely discussed by our men with many of the citizens, who assert that they must resort to every means to obtain their independence, though they do not like the idea of making soldiers of negroes. Prisoners brought in stated that thirty days' furlough was given to every rebel soldier who shot a Yankee prisoner, who might be caught in the act of trying to escape.

On several occasions when government property was destroyed, General Grierson allowed the many poor families around to help themselves to salt, flour, sugar, bacon and molasses. With the exception of the first three days and the last, the weather was delightful. On the morning of the fifth of January, 1865, the command started from Clear Creek, for Vicksburg, in a pelting rain—it was cold and dreary—arriving at the latter place about two o'clock, amid the cheers of thousands, who flocked to the roadside to welcome us. The meeting between Maj.-Gen. Washburne and Brig.-Gen. Grierson was very cordial. In a few days we arrived at Memphis, by the river, from which place I intended to leave for Illinois, to visit my family.

I will now close my lengthy but true narrative by extending my sincere thanks to Brig.-Gen. Grierson, Captain S. L. Woodward, Assistant Adjutant General, for their marked attention and generous appreciation of my services. Also to H. B. Paris, of the Seventh Illinois Cavalry, who is General Grierson's Chief Clerk, for his many acts of kindness, and to his Assistant Clerk, Edward Jones, of the Second Iowa Cavalry, who is a most agreeable comrade.

Conclusion

I will take the liberty of expressing a few opinions respecting the winding up of this rebellion. My long acquaintance with the Southern people, and my knowledge of their dispositions, traits of character, etc., give me some ideas I would like to see carried out.

In the first place, a war is existing between the people of the Northern or Free States and the people of the Southern or Slave States, which has yet to be settled. As there are various opinions as to how this settlement is to be effected, I will confront the public with mine. Two ideas seem to be prevailing among the public—one to subjugate the South, and the other to use mild measures, or, rather, to buy them back. The first two years the war was conducted on the latter plan, and the South, laughing at the very idea, asked, "Have you anymore to give us now than when we seceeded?" The last two years the war has been conducted on the former principle, and the South, with thousands of others, say that you only aggravate them and will make them fight the more desperately. I am of the opinion that, to finally settle this question, and to have a permanent peace, we must have a majority of loyal people in the Southern States.

Now, the question arises how is this to be effected—for the administrations of the Northern and Southern States have been conducted in such ways that the loyalty which was in the Southern States is now nearly extinct. The Confederates would not tolerate a loyal man in their midst, while the Federal authorities would tolerate disloyalty anywhere within their jurisdiction, and, therefore, most of the loyal men who were in the Southern States have gone to the North. Now, when the Southern people lay down their arms, let all the lands in the rebellious States be confiscated, and one hundred and sixty acres of it be given to the head of every white family in the Southern States.

This course, I claim, would largely increase the number of friends of the government, for there are thousands of men in the South who never owned an acre of land. Such a course would not only make friends of them, but would prevent large numbers from becoming paupers and outlaws. The remainder of the lands of the South should be given to actual white occupants who have served three years in the United States army.

In this way there would be placed in the Southern States a majority of loyal men, who would represent themselves in Congress, and enforce the laws at home, and in this way the Southerners would become an enterprising, flourishing, law loving and abiding people. On the other hand, were the Southern people to lay down their arms today, and take the amnesty oath *en masse*, and establish civil law, their first representative would be as vile a rebel as Davis or Wigfall, and they would exterminate within their bounds every loyal man who had given aid or comfort to the Federal government. And who would be the judge to try the secessionist assassin? Who would say to the secession murderer you served him right? On the other hand, to enforce civil law by force of arms would require a standing army of at least two hundred thousand men, and we would have neither a peaceable nor a republican government.

Chickasaw.

LEONAUR

ALSO FROM LEONAUR
AVAILABLE IN SOFTCOVER OR HARDCOVER WITH DUST JACKET

AFGHANISTAN: THE BELEAGUERED BRIGADE *by G. R. Gleig*—An Account of Sale's Brigade During the First Afghan War.

IN THE RANKS OF THE C. I. V *by Erskine Childers*—With the City Imperial Volunteer Battery (Honourable Artillery Company) in the Second Boer War.

THE BENGAL NATIVE ARMY *by F. G. Cardew*—An Invaluable Reference Resource.

THE 7TH (QUEEN'S OWN) HUSSARS: Volume 4—1688-1914 *by C. R. B. Barrett*—Uniforms, Equipment, Weapons, Traditions, the Services of Notable Officers and Men & the Appendices to All Volumes—Volume 4: 1688-1914.

THE SWORD OF THE CROWN *by Eric W. Sheppard*—A History of the British Army to 1914.

THE 7TH (QUEEN'S OWN) HUSSARS: Volume 3—**1818-1914** *by C. R. B. Barrett*—On Campaign During the Canadian Rebellion, the Indian Mutiny, the Sudan, Matabeleland, Mashonaland and the Boer War Volume 3: 1818-1914.

THE KHARTOUM CAMPAIGN *by Bennet Burleigh*—A Special Correspondent's View of the Reconquest of the Sudan by British and Egyptian Forces under Kitchener—1898.

EL PUCHERO *by Richard McSherry*—The Letters of a Surgeon of Volunteers During Scott's Campaign of the American-Mexican War 1847-1848.

RIFLEMAN SAHIB *by E. Maude*—The Recollections of an Officer of the Bombay Rifles During the Southern Mahratta Campaign, Second Sikh War, Persian Campaign and Indian Mutiny.

THE KING'S HUSSAR *by Edwin Mole*—The Recollections of a 14th (King's) Hussar During the Victorian Era.

JOHN COMPANY'S CAVALRYMAN *by William Johnson*—The Experiences of a British Soldier in the Crimea, the Persian Campaign and the Indian Mutiny.

COLENSO & DURNFORD'S ZULU WAR *by Frances E. Colenso & Edward Durnford*—The first and possibly the most important history of the Zulu War.

U. S. DRAGOON *by Samuel E. Chamberlain*—Experiences in the Mexican War 1846-48 and on the South Western Frontier.

LEONAUR

ALSO FROM LEONAUR
AVAILABLE IN SOFTCOVER OR HARDCOVER WITH DUST JACKET

OFFICERS & GENTLEMEN *by Peter Hawker & William Graham*—Two Accounts of British Officers During the Peninsula War: Officer of Light Dragoons by Peter Hawker & Campaign in Portugal and Spain by William Graham .

THE WALCHEREN EXPEDITION *by Anonymous*—The Experiences of a British Officer of the 81st Regt. During the Campaign in the Low Countries of 1809.

LADIES OF WATERLOO *by Charlotte A. Eaton, Magdalene de Lancey & Juana Smith*—The Experiences of Three Women During the Campaign of 1815: Waterloo Days by Charlotte A. Eaton, A Week at Waterloo by Magdalene de Lancey & Juana's Story by Juana Smith.

JOURNAL OF AN OFFICER IN THE KING'S GERMAN LEGION *by John Frederick Hering*—Recollections of Campaigning During the Napoleonic Wars.

JOURNAL OF AN ARMY SURGEON IN THE PENINSULAR WAR *by Charles Boutflower*—The Recollections of a British Army Medical Man on Campaign During the Napoleonic Wars.

ON CAMPAIGN WITH MOORE AND WELLINGTON *by Anthony Hamilton*—The Experiences of a Soldier of the 43rd Regiment During the Peninsular War.

THE ROAD TO AUSTERLITZ *by R. G. Burton*—Napoleon's Campaign of 1805.

SOLDIERS OF NAPOLEON *by A. J. Doisy De Villargennes & Arthur Chuquet*—The Experiences of the Men of the French First Empire: Under the Eagles by A. J. Doisy De Villargennes & Voices of 1812 by Arthur Chuquet .

INVASION OF FRANCE, 1814 *by F. W. O. Maycock*—The Final Battles of the Napoleonic First Empire.

LEIPZIG—A CONFLICT OF TITANS *by Frederic Shoberl*—A Personal Experience of the 'Battle of the Nations' During the Napoleonic Wars, October 14th-19th, 1813.

SLASHERS *by Charles Cadell*—The Campaigns of the 28th Regiment of Foot During the Napoleonic Wars by a Serving Officer.

BATTLE IMPERIAL *by Charles William Vane*—The Campaigns in Germany & France for the Defeat of Napoleon 1813-1814.

SWIFT & BOLD *by Gibbes Rigaud*—The 60th Rifles During the Peninsula War.

LEONAUR

ALSO FROM LEONAUR
AVAILABLE IN SOFTCOVER OR HARDCOVER WITH DUST JACKET

COLBORNE: A SINGULAR TALENT FOR WAR *by John Colborne*—The Napoleonic Wars Career of One of Wellington's Most Highly Valued Officers in Egypt, Holland, Italy, the Peninsula and at Waterloo.

NAPOLEON'S RUSSIAN CAMPAIGN *by Philippe Henri de Segur*—The Invasion, Battles and Retreat by an Aide-de-Camp on the Emperor's Staff.

WITH THE LIGHT DIVISION *by John H. Cooke*—The Experiences of an Officer of the 43rd Light Infantry in the Peninsula and South of France During the Napoleonic Wars.

WELLINGTON AND THE PYRENEES CAMPAIGN VOLUME I: FROM VITORIA TO THE BIDASSOA *by F. C. Beatson*—The final phase of the campaign in the Iberian Peninsula.

WELLINGTON AND THE INVASION OF FRANCE VOLUME II: THE BIDASSOA TO THE BATTLE OF THE NIVELLE *by F. C. Beatson*—The final phase of the campaign in the Iberian Peninsula.

WELLINGTON AND THE FALL OF FRANCE VOLUME III: THE GAVES AND THE BATTLE OF ORTHEZ *by F. C. Beatson*—The final phase of the campaign in the Iberian Peninsula.

NAPOLEON'S IMPERIAL GUARD: FROM MARENGO TO WATERLOO *by J. T. Headley*—The story of Napoleon's Imperial Guard and the men who commanded them.

BATTLES & SIEGES OF THE PENINSULAR WAR *by W. H. Fitchett*—Corunna, Busaco, Albuera, Ciudad Rodrigo, Badajos, Salamanca, San Sebastian & Others.

SERGEANT GUILLEMARD: THE MAN WHO SHOT NELSON? *by Robert Guillemard*—A Soldier of the Infantry of the French Army of Napoleon on Campaign Throughout Europe.

WITH THE GUARDS ACROSS THE PYRENEES *by Robert Batty*—The Experiences of a British Officer of Wellington's Army During the Battles for the Fall of Napoleonic France, 1813 .

A STAFF OFFICER IN THE PENINSULA *by E. W. Buckham*—An Officer of the British Staff Corps Cavalry During the Peninsula Campaign of the Napoleonic Wars.

THE LEIPZIG CAMPAIGN: 1813—NAPOLEON AND THE "BATTLE OF THE NATIONS" *by F. N. Maude*—Colonel Maude's analysis of Napoleon's campaign of 1813 around Leipzig.

www.ingramcontent.com/pod-product-compliance
Lightning Source LLC
Chambersburg PA
CBHW032018090426
42741CB00006B/644